Tracy

Thanks for reading
my book

Wishing you all the
best

Michael Annetta

THE SCIENCE OF CREATING WEALTH™

Dr. Michael Schuster

Published by: Schuster's Performance Coach, Inc.
9312 E. Raintree Drive, Scottsdale, Arizona 85260

SECOND PRINTING

ISBN 978-0-9815152-0-5

The Science of Creating Wealth™

This book is dedicated to those professionals who are in search of truth. It is dedicated to my mentors and role models, alive and dead, who have passed on the truths that I have written within these page via private communications, seminars and books; who have left a path for many of us to discover and follow, should we choose.

Wealth is simply abundance – nothing more, nothing less. Money, as is time, and everything in existence, is energy. Once a person understands and practices the principles I have found and want to share as the basic underlying truths of life; then, this book and the freedom it can bring, the freedom to become a more fully complete, alive human being, can be claimed.

I am indebted to my father and mother, Edward James and Mary Ellen Schuster for guiding me in my life pursuits. Also, to Elliot Simon, to Charles Classon, to Jacob Needleman and Robert Fritz; to Abraham Maslow and Albert Einstein who I have studied and revered, and all who have pursued truth in their lives and left a path for me, and I hope you, to follow. I walked in their footsteps and followed the paths they left. I ended up spending my life helping professionals, like you, to become more free to be the person God intended you to be.

In the end, this book is dedicated to you. If you choose

to take control of your life, then, you must start with money. A lifetime of experience and thousands of clients tells me that when you take control of your money and your time, you are taking responsibility for your life. Your life will change and in a dimension that you now can't totally comprehend unless you have already done this work.

If you don't take responsibility for your life, who will? You are two-natured: You have a physical nature, and you have a spiritual nature. History and 800 lifetimes have shown that one's spiritual nature doesn't come to the front of your life if you are buried by your physical nature, i.e., money and material possessions. Make your life count. Don't spend your life at the money trough. Learn the principles of wealth in this book and dedicate your life to becoming the best human being that you can become.

The talent, the ability, the potential you have is God's gift to you. What you do with it is your gift to God.

Don't take these statements as shallow words. Your very life is at stake. You only live once. Make it count!

"All wisdom is plagiarism; only stupidity is original."
— **Hugh Kerr**

Forward ■
by Robert Fritz

Money is a hard topic for many people because they have certain craziness about the subject. Their eyes narrow, and they are not quite sure how to think or feel around the topic. Often, they have a conflict of two opposite pulls, both of them wrong. They might feel a little angel floating above their heads warning them about the evils of avarice, while, at the same time, they may have a little devil floating above their heads urging them to pursue mindless greed.

Unlike the many books, such as how to make a killing in the stock market or in real estate or numerous other "get rich quick" schemes, this book is about building the financial capacity to live the life you want to create. And that's the key. It is about creating true wealth and not about trying to become rich. This is an insightful contrast that author, Dr. Michael Schuster, brings home in clear and elegant terms.

Dr. Schuster, himself, is a creative man. He is the foremost innovative dentist in his field, and he has taught generations of dentists how to move from a simple model of tooth repair (the tradition among dentists), to a holistic health approach in which patients are treated from an overall long-term health prospect. The difference for dentists is a radical change of treatment approach; and the difference for patients is that they may add an average of ten additional years to their lives.

The difference is also orientational – from a problem-solving modality (which is how most medical treatment is conceived), to a health-creating modality (in which health and well-being become the goal).

Working to create something you desire, is vastly different from working to get rid of what you don't want. Working toward a long and healthy life, is vastly different from fixing health problems when they show up. Working toward creating wealth, is different from avoiding financial hardships. Wealth is about the human spirit, joined with financial well-being and prosperity. Lust for riches (greed) is about compensating for fear about the future, a false sense of identity, over-indulgence, and narcissistic hopes of self-importance.

What is apparent in the pages of **The Science of Creating Wealth**™ is that it makes sense to create wealth, and it makes no sense whatsoever in pursuing riches. At first, this difference may seem obscure, but as you read this book, you will discover the astute distinction between the two. I remember a moment of revelation years ago, that demonstrated this difference when an organizational "bean-counter" translated the term "generating wealth" into "accumulating wealth." Generating means to create, produce, to bring something into existence, to originate, to make, to cause. What an active verb. To accumulate, means to gather, collect, amass. How relatively passive. Generate gives us the image of growing more and more from an abundant

The Science of Creating Wealth™

universe, while accumulating gives us the image of hoarding from a limited and hostile world.

Dr. Schuster has his own unique approach to the subject of generating wealth. He is creative and practical. He has thought about how to build your capability to generate wealth over time from the multi-dimensional vantage points of external factors (logistics, debt, discipline) to internal factors (the inner workings of your mind, heart, spirit, and soul.) He is talking about principles that he, himself, has practiced for many years with great success. His intent is to share with the reader how he has personally generated wealth in his own life. Through **The Science of Creating Wealth**™, he wants to share a good thing.

You read a book like **The Science of Creating Wealth**™ to learn, and that's what you should expect to do. Become a student, roll up your sleeves, prepare yourself to explore uncharted territory. Even if you have devoured the literature about wealth, read this book with the eye of a beginner. That will put you into the best position to discover the profound lessons it has to teach.

And practice Dr. Schuster's sound advice. Put his ideas into your life, and you will begin to experience the deeper levels of creating wealth in your own life. Let yourself shift from a world of problem solving, reacting or responding to prevailing circumstance, to a world in which you are capable of becoming the predominate creative force in your own life.

The Science of Creating Wealth™

Contents

Acknowledgements ∎

The words and ideas presented in this book come for the most part from my day-to-day work as a coach. Many of my clients are people struggling to gain or re-gain control of their lives. This book draws heavily upon their case histories, professionally but sympathetically presented. This book is about them and their stories, not about me. I dedicate this book first and foremost to my clients.

Everyone has teachers. I have been blessed with some remarkable ones. I will talk about them in due course. For now it is enough to say that my greatest teachers were not the researchers and academics with whom I studied. My greatest teachers have been my clients, my students, and my colleagues. This book could not have been written without the testimony of their success in applying the principles of creating wealth. My students are living proof that these principles work, and the process of creating wealth works!

No one writes a book alone. Many others have helped. I will acknowledge their contributions at the appropriate places. Whenever an author writes, he does so at the risk of appearing to be a know-it-all. I hope it will become clear that I harbor no such illusions or pretensions. Many men wiser than myself have contributed their words and ideas to this little book.

I could not have written a book like this many years ago. **The Science of Creating Wealth**™ is not something to be addressed without long professional and personal experience in this area.

I did not want to write a book "before its time", more ideas and speculation than science. I observed and gathered my findings and waited until now, until the years had proven to me that the principles and practices presented in this book are correct. This work is the result of 35 years of public research, training and coaching in the areas of business development, personal development, and wealth creation. I have conducted thousands of interviews and personal coaching calls. These interviews and calls led me to see that there was a profound need for this kind of book.

I want to especially thank my editor, Philip Flemming, Ph.D., for his help and encouragement in writing this book. To Vicki Smith, The Schuster Center's graphic artist, for her help in the graphic design and layout of this book.

And to my wife, Patti. What can one say about love? Love fosters all creation. If it weren't for love, we wouldn't have been created in the first place. Love is the heart and soul of every human being, and every good thing ever conceived and completed. I am, and will be eternally grateful, to have such a life partner as my wife, Patti.

Finally, I want to thank my team members who I work with everyday. There is no question that I have the most dedicated team. I am profoundly grateful for their support.

The Science of Creating Wealth™

In the end, writing is a very solitary activity. I, and I alone, am responsible for the organization of principles and strategies and structure outlined in this book. I invite and entreat you to take a journey with me. I can promise you that if you study and apply the principles and strategies in this book, your life will take on new dimensions of hope, productivity and wealth. Can you envision that? If that seems to you like too grand a promise then perhaps you are not yet ready to create wealth in your life. Put the book down, and don't read it. But if you are ready for knowledge in your life and ready to become the dominant creative force in your life, then **read, absorb, practice** and **act.** Your life is what's at stake here – your life and the lives of every person in your family and every client or patient, friend or colleague you will interact with for the rest of your life.

> *"With discipline all life's problems can be solved. Without discipline, nothing can be solved or created."* — **Scott Peck**

Dr. Michael Schuster
Scottsdale, Arizona

The Science of Creating Wealth™

Why bother to create wealth in your life? It's a fair question, isn't it? Wealth is not like food and water and shelter. Many people live their lives without any experience of wealth. Even some people with high six figure incomes manage never to understand or experience wealth. Wealth is just not watching money flow through your hands. We need first to get clear on what wealth is.

I often ask my clients what they think wealth will do for them. Here are some of their answers.

"It provides you with peace of mind."

"It will enable you to cultivate and use your mind to become something of value to yourself and your world."

"You will become more of the person you were meant to become."

"It will enable you to create a plan and live by your plan."

"It will allow you to experience greater freedom."

"It will allow you to experience financial freedom. That is when you never have to do

anything you don't want to do for money,
and you never avoid doing something you
want to do for a lack of money."

Those are all excellent answers, and we will have something to say about each of them, but first I want to tell you a DREADFUL STORY.

It's 1923 at the Edgewater Beach Hotel in Chicago, and eight of the world's richest financiers have gathered. These eight men controlled more money than the United States government at that time. They included:

- The president of the largest independent steel company
- The president of the largest gas company
- The greatest wheat speculator on Wall Street
- The president of the New York Stock Exchange
- A member of the President of the United States cabinet
- The richest 'bear' on Wall Street
- The head of the world's largest monopoly
- The president of the Bank of International Settlement

Now without doubt these men controlled vast amounts of money. They were *rich* by anybody's standards, but were they also *wealthy*? What is the difference? If you have lots of money, aren't you both rich and wealthy? Let us look at the sequel, 25 years later. It is a dreadful sequel:

- The president of the largest independent steel company, Charles Schwab, had been living on borrowed money for the five years before he died bankrupt.
- The president of North America's largest gas company, Howard Hopson, went insane.
- The greatest wheat speculator, Arthur Cutton, died abroad, insolvent.
- The president of the New York Stock Exchange, Richard Whitney, was sent to Sing-Sing Penitentiary.
- The member of the President's cabinet, Albert Fall, was pardoned from prison so he could die at home.
- The greatest 'bear' on Wall Street, Jesse Livermore, committed suicide.
- The head of the greatest monopoly, Ivar Krueger, killed himself.
- The president of the Bank of International Settlement, Leon Fraser, also died a suicide.

These biographies suggest that money was not something these very rich men had learned to control or to use to build prosperous and stable lives. They had managed to acquire money but they couldn't manage to keep it. Like a bad marriage, money came into their lives and then left them, with disastrous consequences. They went to jail, they went mad, and they killed themselves trying to hold on to it. What they had was not wealth.

I want to suggest a diagnosis of why these very rich men failed. Individual circumstances varied, and a uniquely stressful economic situation visited the US economy 1929-35, but their letters and diaries reveal that none of them were functioning from a creative orientation toward life. They were from the beginning reactive and they became ever more reactive to the unhappy world around them.

This will become one of the major themes of the book but I want to preview it now. Creators never stop creating. People who are creating wealth never stop creating it. Reactors can manage to make good things happen, but then they always see their results reversed. Money comes into their lives, but then it leaves. While creators understand that they must continue to create their whole life, a reactors' energy seems to drain away when they've reached their goal.

Less than 10% of the population of the richest nation in the history of mankind will ever create enough wealth to support a comfortable lifestyle without working... only 10%! Economists marvel at this number, but wealth and income studies keep supporting it. Why can't a rich nation support a wealthier citizenry?

The area that I have spent the majority of my life studying is management and leadership training for professionals. I can tell you that even less than 10% of professionals will ever be able to retire on anything close to the income they had when they were in practice. And many of these are doctors who earned $25M to $60M in their lifetime of business!

The Science of Creating Wealth™

Retrenchment and forced economies are the realities of their retirement.

These individuals had professional expertise, but they lacked knowledge. They had not learned the microeconomics of businesses they have run. They had not learned the principles of creating wealth, and they had not organized them into a useful plan of action.

There are many reasons why professionals don't create wealth in their lives. Everyone who fails to achieve wealth or financial independence has his own story, or more often, his own excuses for why he did not achieve wealth. Some people call these *"the money myths."* I'd like to write now about a few of the most common. Understanding money myths will give you a clearer answer to the question with which we began: Why build wealth?

"Money isn't important!" I remember lecturing to a group in Atlanta about 10 years ago. As I was beginning to outline the importance of wealth in everyone's life, a doctor in the audience raised his hand and said, *"I'm getting a little uncomfortable with all this money talk. I'm really not that interested in money."*

I immediately stopped the lecture and went down the isle and started a dialogue with him. I wanted to understand the man's attitude toward money. My first question asked about his family.

"OK, I understand, you're not that interested in money. But do you have family responsibilities?"

"Oh yes," he said, "I have three children."

I asked their names and ages. They were all still young children, and from the way he spoke about them it was clear he was very proud of his family.

"That's great," I said, "but let me ask you something. Please tell me who is going to feed them, clothe them, educate them, if you can't because you're not interested in money?"

He looked away and didn't answer. I then asked another question. "How much have you saved for their college educations?"

No answer again.

"Have you saved or invested any money for your own future, you know, for your retirement?"

"No," he said. "Not yet."

The conversation was beginning to feel like an negative interrogation, so I broke it off at this point. I wasn't trying to embarrass the man, but his thinking about money was so horribly wrong. He was living a complete and total lie about the importance of money in his life. He really believed that money didn't matter, or as he actually told me after the lecture, that there was something "bad" about pursuing money.

"Money is evil." Think about trying to operate a business while believing that creating wealth is bad! Could there be a more dysfunctional money myth than this? I wish I could tell you that almost no one entertains this view, but many professionals do. I know, because they tell me so. Many doctors and dentists actually harbor the belief that money-making is something evil. No wonder they never manage to achieve financial independence! They see it as something unworthy or bad.

Think about this. Money either serves you or you serve money. You are the master or the slave of money. *"Money isn't important"* or *"money is evil"* are beliefs of people who are not masters of their money. They are the beliefs and concepts of people who are fearful about money and have no idea how to control it.

We cannot be afraid of money. This is the attitude that underlies all of the myths about money. Beliefs are things that are in our control. Beliefs and concepts are things we can change. It is up to you to decide whether you are going to take control of money in your life or whether money is going to control you the rest of your life. Your choice.

Many professionals, especially young professionals, believe that what you produce, or the amount of your compensation, will make you wealthy. They think that this is the key to controlling money and creating wealth. Sadly, they are in for a rude awakening at some point in their lives. You can produce hundreds of thousands of dollars annually and yet accumulate nothing. I see this all too often. When professionals realize that producing more is not going to be the answer, the fear of having no control over money returns. No wonder so many people are afraid and end up lying to themselves about what money is or isn't in their lives.

About six years ago, I attended a three-day Berkshire-Hathaway annual meeting on the invitation of a client and friend who I helped become a multi-millionaire. This professional had created financial independence for himself in just nine years using the principles and strategies and process that I had taught him. The keynote speaker was, of course, Warren Buffet. Mr. Buffet started out by asking the audience for questions. The first question was posed by a woman in her mid-forties. She asked *"Mr. Buffet, what's the difference between being rich and being wealthy?"* I'll never forget his response. *"Rich people never have enough,"* he said, *"while wealthy people always have enough. Wealth is a state of mind."*

He paused and added one more comment, *"Rich people make this mistake: They focus on the 'making of money' but not on creating wealth."*

Remember our "Dreadful Story" of the eight richest men in the U.S.? Warren Buffet could have been talking about them. Those men were focused on making money, but never took the time to train their minds with the strategies and structure required to keep what they had made. They jumped from one risky venture to another until they ran out of luck. They never learned to put their money where they wouldn't lose it and where it would compound over time to create stable wealth. The vast majority of people, over 90%, have the same problem. All their time, energy and effort is spent making money, not keeping it. They remain slaves to a life in which the goal is at best financial survival.

Those who say, *"I'm just trying to survive,"* live in fear. They are overly competitive and overly critical, and most of all, they live their lives fueled with negative energy. Fear ensures that they will not attract wealth or positive opportunities into their lives.

If opportunities do present themselves, people who are angry and fearful cannot embrace them as opportunities. They remain where they are, struggling, working harder, yet becoming more frustrated; on a perpetual downward spiral. Fear, frustration and stress affect their health. They find themselves becoming incapable of forming truly healthy, lasting relationships with others. Do you recognize the syndrome? Fear can and will prevent you from learning, implementing and creating wealth.

We attract into our lives, at every level of our lives, the energy we give out. We also see everything in our lives from our own perspective, with habits of thought and emotion that we have developed over our lifetime. Habits, thought and emotions are a structure of their own. This is a very important point to keep in mind. I am absolutely convinced that it is our "energy" – the positive or negative vibes that we give off – that makes all the difference in our lives.

Many people want to believe that it is what they do for a living, or the amount of professional technical knowledge they have, that will make all the difference. Our prisons hold many people with Ph.D.'s and Master's degrees. Unfortunately, the world is littered with educated derelicts.

It isn't a question of whether you have energy and emotion in your life. Unless you are a rock, you do! The question is whether your energy is positive and creates and sustains life, or whether it is negative and rejects and destroys life.

If the world senses that you are a person dominated by negative energy, creating wealth will be very, very difficult for you. Building wealth for yourself is a two-way transaction. The world must also receive something of value in return for the wealth you are given. You must make and give something of real value to the world. But angry, fearful people want to take, not give. Emotionally they want to cheat, taking but giving nothing in return. The world does not welcome or reward such people with wealth or happiness.

Scarcity is a state of mind and wealth is a state of mind. Buffet reminded us of this a few pages ago. Scarcity and wealth create themselves from the choices we make and how the world reacts to them. Choose to be wealthy, choose to deal with the world in a giving positive way and the world will reciprocate. Choose scarcity and the world will react to you in a different way.

Think about it as if it were a *"build it and they will come"* story. Program your mind for wealth and abundance. Live, breathe, act, think, and feel abundance and wealth, and it will come to you.

Too many people associate being wealthy with having money and sell their souls in the blind pursuit of money. Those who are wealthy have an abundance of health, good relationships, joy, peace, happiness, acceptance and love in their lives. These are reasons why we want to create wealth in our lives. ■

The Science of Creating Wealth™

CHAPTER 1 ■
Who Can Create Wealth?

Think about this statistic. If you are a professional or a small business owner, over the lifetime of your business you will collect somewhere between $25M and $6OM or more in current dollars. That's a lot of money flowing through your hands. Your business is a cash flow machine. It's an oil well with you as the prime pump. You may never have looked at your business in this way, but it's the truth. Think about your business as a cash flow machine.

Every person has patterns with money: How they make and spend and save and invest it. It's important to understand your own patterns with money. You can't control what you don't understand. Every person has a complicated relationship with money. Complicated and often conflicted. I did, you do, everyone does. There is no person alive who does not have strong beliefs and feelings about money. Do you understand why you have the beliefs and feelings you do about money? I am going to help you understand your relationship with money and, if necessary, change it.

You already know this. Money doesn't come into your life or leave it without rhyme or reason. There are certain principles and processes that govern how money is acquired.

You must learn and apply these principles and structures in your life. If you do, you will achieve wealth and financial freedom. In twelve years or less you can secure a life of abundance. If you do not learn these principles, you will never be able to create wealth and abundance in your life.

The Science of Creating Wealth™ is based on these principles. These principles apply everywhere and to everyone. It is a science that is 100% predictable, 100% reliable, and 100% achievable by anyone who chooses to create wealth.

Here is something you may not yet realize. There is more opportunity for creating wealth from your practice or your business than from any other investment you might make. No other investment is a safer or a surer way to create wealth than an investment in your own business. Here's why. Let me give you another statistic: you will have the opportunity to save (on a tax-deferred basis) $60,000 to $200,000 per year, every year, once your business has reached $800,000 in gross revenues. Investing this money wisely – without emotional baggage, without bad advice, without interference – with a sound structure – can lead you to financial freedom in as little as 120 months. Your age, the time you begin, where you are located, what profession you are in, your background and history – all of these matter less than your desire, the principles and structure you put into your life to create wealth.

You are either on the road to creating wealth or you are not. What does being on the road to wealth mean? There are no absolute benchmarks, but a good rule of thumb looks for a stable rate of growth in your net worth. Have you been growing your investments at a rate of at least $100,000 per year? If you haven't, why haven't you?

Since our topic is about creating wealth, let me say a few things about my own experience with creating wealth. To the extent that I've gained mastery in **The Science of Creating Wealth**™, I have done so in the only way that anyone can. I have learned **The Science of Creating Wealth**™ by actually creating tangible results for myself.

For more than 35 years, I have investigated and practiced the principles and process you will learn in this book. Once I had proven to myself that these principles and processes work, I began to teach them to my colleagues. I began sharing these principles with others because I saw so many of my friends and colleagues suffering and struggling in perpetual survival mode. A mentality of scarcity impoverished their lives despite the fact that they were living in a "sea of money".

I had the opportunity to conduct seminars at some prestigious professional institutes and universities. In Q&A's with the participants – over 95% of whom were still practicing – I was astonished to discover that the majority were still experiencing enormous frustration. They just could not figure out how to apply their professional expertise in the day-to-day business of dentistry, medicine, law, optometry, or chiropractic. What was the source of their frustration? Why couldn't they apply the same intelligence and discipline to their business that made them technically so proficient?

For years now, I have had requests to share these principles of creating wealth with people I did not know personally. I became motivated to do so by a vision of what sharing these principles could accomplish. Individuals and their organizations could be empowered to take their destinies into their own hands. They could create lives and businesses that represent their true values and aspirations. They would no longer be held back by trying to run a business in an atmosphere of scarcity and survival thinking.

I am not the first person to discover and write about these principles of creating wealth. A good friend of mine is the author Robert Fritz, who has written several books about creating the life you want. Before I met Robert, I had intuitively found my own path to creating wealth. Once I had met and worked with Robert, I was able to clarify and better articulate my intuitions. Robert speaks about how our deeply ingrained patterns of thought and action, what he calls our "structures", determines how we deal with everything in our life including money. Some structures seem inevitably to bring us to successful outcomes, and others have the opposite result.

One of the best ways to determine which structures lead to success, I realized, was to study people who were already conspicuously successful in creating wealth. When the same structures show up again and again in the lives of very successful people, we realize it is not by accident. I studied successful people and the principles they followed in creating their wealth. Who then can create wealth? The good news is that anyone can. Anyone who follows these same principles and structures.

The principles and structures we will discuss have proven themselves many times and in many ways. Over the past 30 years my team and I have evaluated more than 10,000 small professional businesses. These businesses divided into two distinct classes…

- **those that were creating wealth and abundance, and,**
- **those that weren't.**

When some of the businesses that weren't creating wealth asked us to help them change, we looked first at the structures controlling and limiting their businesses. Without exception, when they were willing to make changes in these structures, they saw significant progress toward the creation of wealth.

Those who create wealth think differently than those who do not. This is a simple, but profound point. My purpose in writing yet another "money book" is to share with you why this is. People who create wealth follow the same principles that you can follow. Following these principles will produce the same results for you and change your life forever.

My hope in sharing this information with you is that you will use it to transform your life. Have no doubts that you can do this! You can take this information and apply it to your own business and life. You can make the changes you need to make. I can assure you that those who have applied these principles to their business and their lives have without exception developed into the human beings they truly wish to be.

Too many individuals are limited not only by their thinking but also by their inability to change. They want to change from a harried, overstressed, survival-based person into a human being not limited by a self-imposed fear of scarcity and a bad relationship with money. They want to change, but they don't know how. My job is to show you how to make the changes that lead to success and wealth.

In simplest terms, by moving towards *creating* and away from *reacting,* you can change your life. You can adopt a creative approach to your life regardless of your present circumstances. My message to you is that if you apply these creative principles to your personal and business life, you will see for yourself that a life inspired by creativity is a far more powerful and meaningful life than a life pre-occupied with reacting to problems and scarcities.

Can you create success while pre-occupied with scarcity and focused on problems? I suppose it's possible, but my observations, studies, and analyses over the last 35 years suggest that is totally the wrong path to take. Think about this. If you want to succeed, why not take the path that has already led many people to prosperity? Why follow a path by which only one or two may have managed to succeed only to see their apparent success reverse itself?

I've seen many lives transformed by learning to apply these principles to the creation of wealth. Achieving wealth and abundance won't transform you into a different person. It simply allows you to become more of the person you truly are. If you are a warm, kind, gentle person, you'll see these personal qualities amplified. If you have strong professional skills and abilities, no matter what your profession, you will become better at what you do professionally.

With credit to the contributions of my friends and colleagues Robert Fritz, Peter Senge and others, I would like to share with you the foundational principles of creative living. You are free to apply them to anything of great importance in your life; but, my focus in this book will be on the creation of wealth. ■

The Science of Creating Wealth™

CHAPTER 2 ■

Discovering What You Want To Create

Like most of you, I had to work very hard to put myself through professional school. Coming out of school, my first thought was to establish myself. In building a new practice, you expect to put in long hours. Whatever it takes, right? But I found myself becoming far too busy. I was burying myself, almost literally, in my work. I felt confused and disoriented – and then I became physically ill. Yes, I was starting to make good money, but I had moved into a permanent *reactive-responsive* mode, driven by my patients' needs for the immediate solutions to their self-defined problems. I ended up in the hospital.

It was a defining moment in my life. The doctors initially thought I had had a heart attack, but thankfully it turned out to be an ulcer. In those days they kept you in the hospital for several weeks. I had some time to think and I used it to figure out that something was terribly wrong. I was 28 years old, lying in a hospital bed with a tube down my throat and culturing a fine peptic ulcer. Can you picture the scene? My three little daughters, three to five years old, came to visit me. *"What's wrong, Daddy?"* Something was desperately wrong.

I knew I was on the wrong track and barreling along in

the wrong direction, but I had no idea how to correct it. My father, a philosopher and teacher, asked me to read a book by Mortimer Adler. Two chapters into the book I read a statement that would change my life. Adler wrote;

"Act AS IF and you will become it."

Thankfully I had some time to reflect on what that meant. Act as if you are something and you will become it. You *will* become it.

That stimulated me to ask a defining question of my life: what exactly was it that I wanted to become? I knew where I was. I knew my current reality. I was sick, overweight, losing my dream, not showing much care for my family, and probably doing a disservice to my patients by not offering them more. That's what and where I was, no doubt about it. That was the truth about myself that I faced. But what did I want to become? What kind of life and practice did I want create for myself? By merely reacting to my patients' problems, I had created a reactive, problem solving practice, not a practice and a life based on what I truly wanted.

At that moment I resolved to change. I would stop being a reactive, problem-solving person and become a creative, future-focused person. In that moment of discovery I also realized two things that moved me further into the creative process. Since I am a dentist, my thoughts were focused on dentistry and my practice. I realized that...

- **what my patients *wanted* was *no dentistry***

or as little dentistry as possible, but,

- what they truly **wanted** was to be healthy,
  free of disease, needles, drills, pain
  and distress.

I made a fundamental choice at that moment, to organize my entire life and practice around pursuing health, not reacting to disease. I decided to work only on a long-term basis with those patients who wanted to be healthy, in the fullest sense of health and wellness. I wanted my patients to pursue a complete state of physical, mental, emotional and spiritual wellness; one free from disease and pain of course, but also one sound and vigorous in all areas as the result of proper diet, exercise and stress reduction.

I knew it had to start with me. It wasn't easy at the beginning, but I modified what I ate and began to eat healthy. I started to run daily, and gradually got myself up to an average of better than 5 miles a day. I ran an average of 30 miles a week for 26 years. Today, I walk 7 hours a week with heavy hands. Though the gym wasn't a fun place for me, I worked out almost every day on my strength and flexibility. In sum, I began to act **as if** I were healthy and fit. I changed the structure of my life regarding diet, exercise and stress reduction.

My goal from the beginning was a healthy life, but at first, I didn't have a vision of what a healthy life looked like. I saw only the unhealthy person I was, not the healthy and fit person I wanted to become. Having a picture of the future I wanted to create was crucial. Once I had it, once I could see myself acting as a healthy and fit person, it really wasn't that hard for me to act *as if.* I began to act *as if* every day, and in less than a year I was running marathons in under four hours.

I realized I was succeeding in becoming the healthy person I wanted to be. I was succeeding not because of luck or a super-human willpower or any special talents; but because I was proceeding in the right way, following principles of creating change that would work for me or anyone else. Once I had proven to myself that these principles work, it was time to apply them to my practice, to create the "healthy" practice I wanted.

I began by discussing with my new clients what they wanted most to create in terms of oral health. I would show them a picture of a healthy mouth and then show them a picture of a diseased mouth. We would discuss the attributes of health that were present in the healthy mouth and what was missing or evident in the picture of the unhealthy mouth. After this discussion, I would present the potential client with an invitation. I would say *"I don't know if your mouth is more like the picture of health or if it is more like the picture of disease. The only way we can both know is if we do a thorough examination and discover this together. Would you be interested in pursuing the co-discovery process with me, and then we can co-plan the level of health you aspire to create for yourself?"*

These are the exact words and pictures I used and still use today. Ninety-five percent of all those whom I interviewed in this way said *'yes'* to the process. My practice immediately began to go in a different direction with a decidedly different outcome.

The Science of Creating Wealth™

This was the first time in my professional life that I realized that I could entirely change the structure of what I was doing. I could do it because I had moved from reacting to creating. I could do it because I had discovered the power of what Robert Fritz calls the **Principles of Structural Thinking.** This was in 1970! Once I began to understand the power of this creative process, I saw that I could also apply it in other areas of my life.

Let me write a little more generally about the benefits of creative thinking. First, when you begin to think in a creative way, you become much smarter than you used to be. I don't mean your IQ jumps twenty points and you start getting invited to MENSA parties. What I mean is this. We all have been endowed with **intelligence** to think, with **emotions** to feel, and with a **will** to act. If we think better, with greater clarity, focus, and understanding of how to create what matters most in our lives, then we make better decisions. Better decisions make our lives simpler. For one thing, we aren't always fixing problems we shouldn't have created in the first place. An intelligent person wants a simpler life in this sense. It is a better life. As Aristotle told us 2300 years ago, one of the keys to a happy life is *practical* intelligence.

I was speaking with Robert Fritz about this recently. We agreed that though we both did well in high school and college, (he began to excel in college, consistently on the dean's list, and I began to excel in dental school), we were by no means the most intelligent people in our classes. Yet, we've both created many wonderful things in our own lives and have helped others create lives they would never have had without these principles.

I think the obvious lesson is you don't need great intelligence to succeed. Creating wealth is not about intelligence, it's about principles and structure. The principles of creating wealth in your life are relatively simple. Learn them and practice them and they will work for you. It's a *science* of creating change in the sense that if you take action X, you will get result Y every time. If you want to get great results, study and practice. Remember, you'll never create anything of value unless it truly matters to you.

In another chapter, I will write about why so many people don't take action to create the life they want. There are many people who spend their entire lives in confusion. They never manage to produce any of the results they truly want. It is important for you to know the 'whys' of this: Why 90% of people are stuck and unable to move forward, despite having many talents, capabilities and opportunities.

But first, let me write more about the principles of creating the life you want. ■

CHAPTER 3 ■
Structure Determines Behavior Determines Results

There is a set of principles I first encountered at MIT nineteen years after I began using the Creative Process. These principles gave me the proof and the confidence I needed to go public with my thinking. The basic principle is very simple. Most people, I believe, simply overlook it. Here it is:

Structure determines behavior determines results.

More grammatically and less elliptically, your structures (or systems) determine your behavior, which, in turn, determines the results you get. More than likely, you have not taken the time to reflect on the structures or systems that control your life. To most of us these structures are virtually invisible. We need training to learn to see them, and even then, many of us don't recognize them.

In a culture addicted to the quick fix and satisfied with reacting to events, most of us are not aware how much we are creatures of habit and how often we are controlled by our recurring patterns of behavior. Let me share a story with you.

One morning, a few years ago, I picked up a call at my training center. The call was meant for someone else, but the doctor was eager to speak to me. My conversation with the doctor went something like this:

"Hi Mike. I'm glad you picked up this call. Can we talk about something?"

"Sure," I said.

"I have a problem."

"OK. Shoot, what's your problem."

"I have a cash flow problem", the doctor said.

"OK, so how long have you had this problem?"

"Well," he said, "I think I've had it for as long as I have been in practice."

"And how long have you been in practice?" I asked.

"Eleven years."

"You've had a cash flow problem for **eleven** years?" I asked.

"Yep, for eleven years. For as long as I've been practicing."

What do you think I was thinking as I was listening to this man? *"Structure determines patterns of behavior which determines results."* This professional had established a pattern of behavior in his practice that could not fail to recur! Beneath this pattern of behavior was a structure, a reliable, predictable, repeatable structure, that was creating his unhappy results. In his reactive world, and even with heroic effort, whatever strategies and tools he put in place could only secure a limited and temporary progress. In time, any progress would be reversed because the underlying structure remained unchanged.

No matter how much money this doctor produced, he was still going to have a cash flow problem. He was never going to create financial wealth and abundance in his practice because of a chronic pattern of mismanaging money. This pattern of a lack of money was caused by the structures he had in place in his business concerning money.

Many of you, I'll bet, have seen a business in which billing is slow and collections are poor. There is always going to be a cash flow problem in a business run that way.

We need to think about why our doctor with a cash flow problem fell into this pattern in the first place. Robert Fritz would offer us an answer in terms of *"structures and paths of least resistance"* through life.

Fritz says we are all innately disposed to go through life taking *paths of least resistance.* The definition of the *"path of least resistance"* is a path that we believe will create the least pain and inner conflict for us. Energy moves where it is easiest to go.

The structures we have put into our life and business have evolved consciously or unconsciously, but they define our patterns of behavior and results, our path of least resistance. If we have a structure that says we should use money in a certain way, then money will continue to flow through one's life along that same least-resistance pathway. Similarly, if we have structures that say we should treat relationships or behavioral problems (i.e., alcohol or drug abuse) in certain ways, those structures will dictate the same behaviors again and again.

We will handle money, time and literally everything in our lives in ways that follow the structures we have put into our lives. You have no other alternative than to follow your own path of least resistance. Unfortunately, these least-resistance pathways are not often practical or sound paths. They do not lead to achieving good results like wealth and health.

We lose money because we handle it in ways we are comfortable handling it. We destroy or complicate meaningful relationships because we proceed in ways in which we are most comfortable proceeding. We abuse alcohol or some other substance because we think it actually helps us manage our stress levels and feelings of unhappiness. In short, our structures are not necessarily wise or well-adapted to the world.

Some psychologists are fairly pessimistic about our ability to revamp our basic structures. Fritz and I are realists, not on psychological grounds, but on the basis of what we've seen happen in our own lives and in the lives of our clients. I promise you, you can change the structures that are making certain areas or your life marginally or totally dysfunctional. If the wrong structures with regard to money are impairing your business, you can learn to identify these structures and change them. You can create the wealth in your life that you want.

I'm going to write more about these problems and issues, but it is essential now that you grasp two extraordinary principles. I hope upon reflection they seem obvious to you.

1. **Human beings act and react in accordance with the underlying structures in their lives.**

2. **Some structures are far more deeply rooted than others, but all structures are tractable and malleable.**

The Science of Creating Wealth™

Notice that the first principle mentions both acting and reacting. I want to write more now about reacting and structures. The primary reactive form of thinking is problem solving. Unfortunately, we all have been trained to problem solve, and some of us do it fairly well, but ultimately it is a kind of thinking that leads to structuring our lives and businesses in a way which is inadequate to create what we truly want. With problem solving you move away from what you don't want, but don't move towards what you really, really want.

Why is problem solving inadequate to create the business and life you want? Because when you are problem solving, you are taking action to make something go away. You want *the problem* to disappear from your life. When you are creating, you are taking action to bring something into existence. You are introducing something new – *the Creation* – into your life.

Your intentions are exactly the opposite when you are problem solving than when you are creating.

Working one-on-one with patients and clients for over 35 years, I've seen far too much emphasis on problem solving. Most professionals have learned to think in terms of problem solving. This leads them and their clients to frustration. They bring high energy to their businesses but without results, and they more often experience reversals.

While speaking at a seminar some years ago, this question came from a doctor in the audience. It's one I've heard over and over from those trapped in the wrong structure, a problem-solving, reactive structure. The doctor said, "I've tried to get ahead before and it simply didn't work. I made some progress and then I seemed to go backwards. How do I make progress and then hold on to it?" In another seminar, another professional asked a very similar question: "I worked with a consultant and for a little while I made some gains. But then he went away. What do I need to do to make my gains last?" You see the common thread in these questions. These people put their faith in problem solving. Problem solving suppresses the problem for a while but it always returns. It returns because problem solving did not address the underlying structural problem and did not create a new structure to supplant the dysfunctional one.

Another comment I often hear at seminars is this: "I've tried to save and invest before, and I ended up losing a great deal of money." You can see that investing is a recurring problem for this kind of person. Instead of a cash flow problem, he has a, **"what do I do with the cash"** problem. When he has an amount to invest, he reacts with problem solving. He's asking himself, "Where can I put this money so it won't be a problem for me?" This individual, like millions of others, has failed to discover a sound investment structure; one that will consistently produce returns with NO LOSSES!

I can't estimate the percentage of individuals who save or invest reactively. All I can say is this: When I've visited or coached or had dialogue sessions with professionals, I can count on the fingers of one hand those who have learned to think creatively rather than reactively about money. Those who think creatively have learned or created an investment strategy that produces consistent, long-term results and gains.

I have said that I was originally guided to this path of creating by my father and Alfred Adler. I was also introduced to the teachings and philosophy of Abraham Maslow at about the same time. I was intrigued by his studies not of diseased people, but of the healthiest people he could find. I listened to hours of Maslow's interviews with clients and to many of his lectures. I read just about everything he wrote and much of what other people have written about him.

What Abraham Maslow discovered was this: Healthy people operated from structures that were different from those in which less healthy and less successful people relied. He discovered that their orientation was quite different. Maslow often focused on why more people didn't evolve, grow or become more, as he called it, "self-actualized."

I was more fascinated by the fact that the healthiest people he studied had a different orientation towards their life and work. The importance of orientation is something I have felt keenly about at different times of my life. Especially as I have become more aware of my own patterns of behavior and learned to observe the underlying structures in my own life.

Healthy people, truly health-oriented people, have a visibly different orientation to life than those who are not as healthy. You could best describe their orientation as a disposition to create rather than to react or respond or problem solve.

I've been fortunate to have as close professional and personal friends some very creative people. L. D. Pankey, F. Harold Wirth, Peter E. Dawson, Robert Fritz, Bob Lee and Robert Barkley were, and have been, mentors and friends in my life. Being around these people and witnessing firsthand their creative orientation towards their profession has proven to me, like nothing else, the power of the **Creative Process.** A **Creative** orientation towards life achieves so much more than a **Problem Solving** orientation.

Why are so many people wed to a *Problem Solving* orientation? One answer is that they have never been exposed to the alternative. Individuals who have never studied the *Creative Process* pursue problem solving as their only option. They've learned that a *Problem Solving* orientation leads to continuous exasperation and frustration. They've learned that one problem leads to the next, and there is never a sense of accomplishing what truly matters most. *"But what choice do I have?"* they will ask you. *"What other way of doing things is possible?"*

I understand this frustration and even desperation. You know what you're doing isn't working but you don't know how to fix it. I often ask my clients, *"If we solve all your problems, then what do you have?"* The response is always, *"I don't know."*

The problem solving orientation is a kind of waste management approach to fixing your life and business. You think you can fix everything by hauling all your problems to the dump. Well, that does empty the trash bins for a while. But then they fill up again. They fill up again because you have not fixed the structures that keep generating problems in your life. Pretty soon you are buried in trash again. You see that this approach goes nowhere. It leads to frustration. It leads to continual battles and no victories. It leads to a life that feels like it is always working against the grain. Money will remain a central problem in your life unless you transform your relationship with money by changing how it flows in and out of your hands.

A conversation I had with Russell Ackoff of the Wharton School of Business explored the differences between the *Creative Process* and the *Problem Solving* orientation. Dr. Ackoff focused on the structural thinking that is at the heart of the *Creative Process*. He said, *"Structure doesn't solve problems, it dissolves them. Problems are dissolved as a by-product of the process of intentionally creating what you want."*

Let me leave you with this suggestion. If you are trying to solve the problem of not having enough money at home or in business, it isn't that you are in the wrong profession. It may not be because you aren't making enough money. It's because the structures you've created in your life, your basic life and business orientation, are not those conducive to creating wealth. You are stuck in an orientation of reacting to money problems. You can change this. In the next chapter, I will begin to set out the key steps to creating wealth. ∎

The Science of Creating Wealth™

CHAPTER 4 ■
The Creative Process

You have a choice. You can choose to orient your life around the problems in your life and in the lives of those you care for and serve, or you can orient your life around creating what is most important to you and to those you care for and serve. This is a real choice. Think about it.

The fundamental principles and steps in creating anything are universal. By that I mean they can be applied by anyone to anything in any life that you want to create. The basics of the Creative Process are simple and precise.

When I talk about creating wealth and explain the basics, many people say to me, *"I'm already doing this."* My response to them is a question. *"If you truly understood the process of creating wealth, wouldn't you already be on the path to achieving it?"* Let's not kid ourselves. Time to look in the mirror and see what's really there. Be honest with yourself. If you truly understood this process and were able to apply it, you would already have done so in many areas of your life. Maybe you have in one area of your life intuitively, but can't duplicate it in other areas because you don't understand the principles of creating.

It is because of the lies we tell ourselves that we get

into the most trouble. We think we know, but we don't. For me, it has always been only after I was forced to admit that I didn't know something that my mind opened up to a different way of thinking. The Creative Process is a different way of thinking.

I'm going to outline the steps of the Creative Process and make a couple of comments regarding each step from my own very personal perspective.

- **Step 1: Begin with the End Result that you wish to create. Envision or picture the future you want.**

At first this may seem too general, but later it will become specific.

Picture what you want. I've said for over 30 years that one of the easiest things to deal with is money. Money isn't an abstraction or an idea, it is a real tangible thing. You can see it, you can count it, you can save or spend it, you can even stuff it in your mattress. My point is that you can easily envision the financial future you want. When I speak of wealth, what I am referring to is an abundance of money. You have an abundance when having more than you need for the basics and enough to plan for the future you want.

The future you want to create and why you want to create that future are things personal and unique to you. You can't set out to create something just because someone else said you should. Our schools have done a miserable job in teaching us to envision the life we truly want to create. They have been busy showing us *how* we should conform to certain

The Science of Creating Wealth™

pre-set archaic mindsets; not allowing our own creativities and abilities to recognize the path and process we individually choose for our own wealth and happiness.

Creating wealth is a very interesting exercise in creation. At first glance, it seems simple enough; but it can't be that simple, or there would be many more than just 10% of the population (in the richest country in the history of mankind) who could stop working and still have enough passive income to maintain the lifestyle they had while working.

I personally, find wealth and money to be fascinating topics. Let me share with you what I think is an insight. After years of observation and research involving thousands of professionals, I've come to the conclusion that acquiring money should never be treated as the end result. Money is always best seen as the means to other ends, ends such as:

1. **Securing financial freedom.**
2. **Engaging in a profession or conducting a business for its own sake and not just profits.**
3. **Having peace of mind that the future is secure.**
4. **Being in control of money.**
5. **Being able to do what matters most rather than having money dictate the terms of your life.**

Besides wealth or abundance in a financial sense, there are many other aspects of your future you can and should envision. Knowing what you want is the major prerequisite of

Step One. If you don't know what you want and don't have a crystal clear picture of it, it's doubtful that you will have enough energy to create it.

I find that some people are comfortable having others set goals for them. This is not a good start to the Creative Process. Doing things because you think you should or because someone told you to, is not the way to create the life YOU want.

Many people I meet are not even sure why they went into their profession or created their business in the first place. It's hard to be enthusiastic about a choice you really don't remember making freely and consciously.

In my own case, I have found great effectiveness in using the Creative Process when I am clear about what I want to create and why I want to create it. In fact, I usually make a list of all the things I'm going to get as a result of the process. Some people refer to these as the *"payoffs"* of the Creative Process.

Right now I would like you to take a few minutes and write down on the inside back cover of this book what you believe are going to be the big *payoffs* when you create wealth. Write down that list and please don't let anyone, myself included, influence your thinking. The list can be long or short; but in general, the more reasons you have to create, the more likely you will create.

- **Step 2: Know your current reality.**
  Know where you are now.

This is the most difficult step for most of the people I work with in the Creation Process. It is difficult for all of us to see ourselves as we really are. I remember Peter Senge saying *"We judge others by what they do. We judge ourselves by what we think. That's how we become legends in our own minds."* Only those who are truthful with themselves and about themselves will ever create.

It is always a humbling experience to be brutally honest with ourselves. Being able to take stock and know exactly what is real in our lives is a very difficult thing. We do not see ourselves as others see us. We don't see ourselves objectively. The skills of the objective observer can be developed but not without difficulty. All creators need to learn to do this as an essential step in the Creative Process.

The bigger the *blind spot* with regard to ourselves and the truth about ourselves, the more difficult it will be to become a creator rather than a reactor to life and money.

Years ago, I read a book by the Bennett brothers. In fact, it's one of my favorite little books. They first entitled it **Control Theory,** then in a later edition **Reality Theory.** Well, reality is all about the truth. So, I think they should have chosen a third title, **Truth Theory.** That's how I teach it, as Truth Theory. Reality is truth! My friend, Jacob Needleman suggests that the truth is an acquired taste, and indeed it is.

I find that a surprisingly large number of people have a totally distorted view of their reality, especially about themselves. Some perceive themselves perfect and spend a great deal of time telling others how great and perfect their lives and businesses have become. They often use clichés to describe their current reality and to suggest that they really aren't that interested in money. When, in truth, they are sometimes desperate. Other people are too hard on themselves and have internalized some deeply negative views of their situation. They perceive their world too dark, entertaining an excessively pessimistic view of their reality.

In my own case, I admit I have had to work at the discipline of facing current reality. Self-scrutiny is not something that comes easily or naturally to me. I have to sit down by myself and reflect and really look at myself. *"To thine own self be true"*, says the sage, but who is this person I see in the mirror and what are his true circumstances? What in his life is truly guiding the patterns of behavior that seem to forever recur in life?

For me to begin creating something, regardless of whether it is a book like this one, a lecture, a seminar, a building, a business, a wealth or health program, I must begin with the exact truth of where I am at this moment. That is the first picture I need to create in my mind (in as much detail and clarity as possible). Once I have that picture, then I can re-focus and try to get a second picture, a vivid picture of what it is I want to create. Now, I can go back to the first picture and put it side-by-side with the second. One picture of where I am. One picture of where I want to go. One picture of current reality, one picture of the future I want to create. Back and forth I go,

The Science of Creating Wealth™

noticing all of the changes I need to make to go from current reality to desired future. This is how I have trained my mind to think. I block out everything else and focus on these two pictures. As I try to gauge the distance from current reality to what I want to create, I also keep asking myself why I want to create this future.

I'm getting a little ahead of myself in explaining the Creative Process, but I want to explain to you why it's so necessary to get a true fix on your current location. The Creative Process sets in motion a plan for a journey from where you are, to where you want to be. It's in part a set of directions for visiting every place you must visit on your journey if you're to reach your final destination. Imagine trying to plan a journey when you don't have a starting point? Try to get directions to anywhere when you don't know where you are!

I find in my interviews and discussions with patients and clients, many do not really know where they are. *I don't want to call this a studied avoidance, much less a fatal flaw, because the disciplines of facing the current reality and envisioning the future you want are skills anyone can acquire, if you have the desire.* But you have to know about them and want to acquire them. Both skills are required in the Creative Process. Each step must be completed within the process.

- **Step 3: Build Structural Tension by comparing the picture of your current reality with the picture of the future you want.**

This step has been raised to a fine art by Robert Fritz. Robert, who is a musician, was perhaps led toward the idea of Structural Tension by his fondness for counterpoint in Renaissance and Baroque compositions. Two independent melodic ideas develop simultaneously that react to one another, ultimately tending towards greater harmony; yet, in the process generating strong tensions as they play against one another. It is easier to hear this than explain it in words. Listen to some Johann Sebastian Bach.

In the Creative Process we are similarly trying to develop or elaborate two separate themes or visions. We want the themes to hold tension against one another and so highlight their differences. We need to carefully elaborate both our visions of current reality and of the future we want. Otherwise, if either vision is weak or distorted, the tension we want and seek to create will not be created.

This is a very important point and I'm going to risk repeating myself. If you aren't truthful in setting out your current reality, if you fudge it or lie to yourself or tell yourself anything but the truth, then that side of the composition will be false and off-key. Likewise, if you are not crystal clear about the future you want, that side of the composition will play badly. The Structural Tension needed to move you forward won't develop unless both sides of the composition are strong and true.

Painters, musicians, and writers create works of art because they want to create. That wanting comes from a sense of their creative vision being unrealized. The contrast of the unfinished canvas and their vision of the final picture enables them to complete the creative process. The Structural Tension that arises, drives them to explore new ways, innovative actions and strategies, to realize their vision. There is inevitably a lot of trial and error. Not every action moves them toward what they want, but because of the force of Structural Tension, they keep moving forward toward what they want. You can do the same. Everyone can. As Robert Fritz advises us in one of his books, *"treat your life like a work of art"*.

I know that Structural Tension works because that is exactly how I invented the Business Development Process I launched in the early 1970's. Structural Tension is what drove me to create the **Dental Fitness Program.**

I began with a vision of what I wanted. I wanted to create health for myself and my clients, (and I wanted to create wealth for myself and my future). My current reality at that time was that I wasn't living a healthy life and I wasn't creating the financial success I wanted. I was brutally honest with myself about all the specifics. It quickly became clear to me that the traditional ways I had been taught to create health and wealth weren't working for me. I had to innovate to create the changes I wanted. The tension of my unfulfilled vision of health and wealth drove me on, even though I had not read the works of Fritz, Senge and Ackoff, Forester and others. I had been introduced to the concepts and theories of Adler and Maslow, and that was enough to start a frustrated but determined young man moving in the direction of becoming creative and health-centered. If you follow the steps of the Creative Process, the process will work for you whether or not you know the theory.

I created the Business Development Program to transform any business from a production-oriented, reaction-based business into a wealth-creating machine. I created the **Dental Fitness Program** to help my clients move from problem-solving, disease-centered dentistry to a health-centered, more creative orientation in dentistry. Those were my visions. Every process I developed in my Business Development Program, (from money management, to time management, to sales and marketing, to creating team synergy), uses the Creative Process which creates Structural Tension that is designed to drive you toward your goals.

• Step 4: Take Action

If you have performed Steps One through Three correctly, it is almost superfluous to add that you will take action. You cannot stop yourself from taking action if you are inspired by a vision of the future you want and driven forward by Structural Tension. You cannot sit still and passively watch the future you want drift away.

Remember, as you take action, that creating is more a matter of innovation than of simply repeating the party line of what has always been done. Creating is acting in new and different ways. Do not be afraid to go your own way. Don't just follow other people's ropes up the mountain. If you follow somebody up the mountain without thinking on your own, chances are great that you'll end up spending your life climbing the wrong mountain.

As you gain results from what you are doing and make progress towards what you want to create, you will discover that much comes from trial and error. What does not work is often as important as what does work in moving you forward. All you can be completely sure about when you begin is that you want to create a certain result. You know the outcome that you want. By continuing to focus both on the outcome (future picture) and its distance from your current reality you will find that you have plenty of motivation to create what matters most to you.

Creating has its own momentum. Moving forward towards what you want is an action that is its own reward. Regarding the process of creating wealth, I'm often reminded of Buckminster Fuller's statement regarding the necessity of weathering *precessionary events* on the way to achieving our desired outcomes. Fuller stated, *"When you set a goal or outcome and you decide to create it, the 'precessionary events' (those things that happen to you on the way to creating your outcome) are often more important than the outcome itself."*

Remember also, that if you set a goal like accumulating $3M dollars (or whatever the number is) in savings and investments, it's not the mere accumulation of this wealth that is most important, but the kind of person you become in the pursuit of the objective. My little Irish mother, whom I loved deeply, used to say to me, *"Always set goals beyond yourself, so you can grow into yourself."*

I said at the beginning that we all had a choice. Let me reformulate that choice and acknowledge some of its complexity. Among the things we choose are the structures, processes, methods and models that determine our thoughts and actions. We can choose to become creators of the life we truly want or we can choose to remain *reactors* to the circumstances and problems that bind us to our present life. That choice will determine whether you make the transformation toward creating wealth in your life or whether you don't. We can also choose to have meaningful relationships and to contribute to the well being of others. Make those significant choices if they are right for you. Make them today and then let the Creative Process make them a reality in your life. ■

"It matters not how strait the gate,

How charged with punishments the scroll,

I am the master of my fate;

I am the captain of my soul."

— **William Ernest Henley**

This is how the poet William Ernest Henley expresses his belief in the indomitable human spirit. The title of the poem, **"Invictus",** means indomitable or unconquerable. William Faulkner echoed these sentiments in his acceptance speech for the Nobel Prize:

"I decline to accept the end of man. It is easy
enough to say that man is immortal simply
because he will endure... I refuse to accept
this. I believe that man will not simply endure;
he will prevail. Humanity will endure because
each human being can say, 'I am the master
of my fate.'"

Whatever scientific or religious views we accept about the creation of mankind, we must not lose sight of the fact that all individuals create themselves.

We, you and I, are unique creations. We have three faculties that ensure that we can make choices. As I said earlier, we have an **intellect** which allows us to think, we have **emotions** which allow us to feel, and we have a **will** which allows us to take action. We were endowed by the Creator with these abilities, and as a result, we have free will. Free will gives us the power to take charge of our lives. We need not be stuck with what we are now. We can make of ourselves whatever we want to become. You can take charge of your life. You can create the life you want. Believe this. This book will show you how.

My focus in this book is on creating wealth. You can choose to make wealth a part of your life or you can choose to reject it. It's that simple and that powerful of a choice.

Some people don't want wealth and what it would bring into their lives. Their beliefs and emotions won't let them choose wealth. Does that make sense to you? Look at yourself. You either want wealth and what it will bring to you or you don't. You need to know the answer to that question without hesitation. *"Well, maybe."* is not an answer.

It is an unhappy truth that more people are motivated by the fear of loss than the hope of gain. I have not kept track of this statistic, but I'm sure that the majority of people I've worked with were more responsive to losses than to the hope for gains. This is another unfortunate pattern that distinguishes the 90% who react to the present rather than create the future.

There are consequences to not making the choice to create wealth. In my coaching work at The Schuster Center, I meet many professionals in their early 50's and 60's who have done little or no wealth creation. They have prepared very little for the present they now inhabit. As a rule, they aren't broke, but because of lack of planning, saving and preparation, they will have to work until they drop. They are truly "tied to the chair."

Professionals in their 50's and 60's who must work are for this same reason much more likely to become burdens to their children. These people are never going to be able to help their children in ways they want, and in fact, many will end up wards of their children. Professional and small business owners who have had the income to plan for a wonderful life and retirement are especially at risk here.

Many who are dependent on current income in later life are also going to find that they are not free to do the things they want to do or go to the places they want to go. Or, perhaps they can, but only with severe penalties in their lifestyles. They are now stuck in a life they don't want but can't afford to change. I have met far too many older men and women caught in this trap. They end up bitter, unhappy and cynical in their declining years, instead of happy, joyful and at peace with themselves and their life.

The consequences of not choosing to create wealth are profound. Many in later life want to be free to pursue other lifelong interests. Some want to travel and enjoy outdoor recreations. Others want to explore neglected artistic talents. Still, others want to be in a position to give generously to various charitable causes. The small business man who has to work until he drops is never going to have the time, the resources, or the energy to cultivate other interests. He can only watch as his more prudent friends pursue and enjoy their own interests, broadening and enriching their lives.

Growing old without having created wealth is not a wise choice for professionals. A vision of the kind of future that awaits an older professional struggling to get by should scare the living daylights out of younger professionals who continue to overspend in their business and personal life, pay more than their share of income tax, and not save for the future.

"I'll work until I drop!" is a hard and unhappy road to follow and a bitter pill to swallow. Prefer to create wealth now. Create a wealth plan now.

So, does any of this touch home? Have you seen professionals struggling in their declining years to hold on? What do you think about that kind of future? Do you think none of this applies to you? That you can spend and spend today and not worry about tomorrow? Do you imagine wealth creates itself?

Choosing to pursue or reject wealth is a fundamental choice. Aristotle suggested a couple of thousands of years ago that the fundamental choices we make are few, but they set the direction of our lives. We can choose to pursue or reject...

HEALTH   WEALTH   BEAUTY
TRUTH   LONG LIFE

The Science of Creating Wealth™

These, and maybe a few others, are the big choices we will make in our lives. Looking at these big choices and the goals they involve, we are forced to consider what we really want in our lives. Once these big choices are made, then the many secondary choices we must make on a daily or even hourly basis are pretty much settled. Secondary choices must support and align with our fundamental or primary choices. If you choose wealth, then you also accept the many secondary choices that are required in your pursuit of wealth.

In my experience, people who are confused, who vacillate and are unsure of themselves, haven't made the fundamental choices. As I just said, the big choices demand a clear, unambiguous, and unqualified answer. *"Well, maybe."* is not a choice to create wealth or health in your life. *"I think so, provided it's not too hard."* is even worse. This is not a choice and a commitment to create wealth or anything else in your life.

"All good things we gain with pain," said a Greek poet. If you want to create wealth in your life, and if you want it enough, then you don't hedge your commitment with reservations and hesitations about how difficult the struggle may become. You create the path to get there and accept all of the costs involved.

Pause for a minute and reflect on how you treat the money you now make and spend. Do any patterns jump out at you? Do you see yourself in any one of these patterns of behavior?

a. I spend everything I take in every month

and year and a little bit more besides.

b. **I spend everything I make every month, quarter, and year.**

c. **I spend everything except a small portion which I save each month.**

d. **I have a consistent amount that I save or invest each month.**

e. **I created a financial plan some time ago and I have managed to save and invest enough that now I have a passive income about equal to my active income.**

One of these alternatives probably fits you. It is your pattern with money. It is your path of least resistance in financial matters. This is a simple truth about you. There are thousands of books out there telling you how to manage your money, but the majority are completely and totally wrong because they overlook your ingrained patterns and habits with money. You can change your patterns with money, but not if you pretend they don't exist. We just talked about creating new structures and patterns. Remember? It's first a matter of getting a very clear picture of the financial future you want, then being honest about your current situation. And, finally taking action every day to move from where you are now to where you want to be. I hope this sounds familiar. If not, go back and reread the Four Steps in Chapter Three.

As you read this, you may be sitting somewhere on vacation or in a quiet place. You are saying to yourself, "*This is all too simple. There has to be more to it."* My answer is that the creative process is *elegantly simple.* It is we who complicate it. Life is complicated, but we can simplify it with positive, clear thinking and actions.

I chose to create wealth and health and to be true to myself when I was 28. Nine years after I had made these fundamental choices, by the time I was 37, I had created enough wealth that I could have retired and lived on the interest and dividends for the rest of my life. Please don't think I'm bragging. Quite the opposite. I offer myself humbly as living proof that this science works. If I could do it, believe me, you can too!

Sometimes it helps to "bundle" your big choices, because they re-inforce and support one another. When I chose wealth, I also chose health as a fundamental choice and have been living a healthy lifestyle ever since. Health and fitness give you the energy to move your business forward. Everything goes much easier if you are healthy and fit. When I chose wealth, I also chose truth as a fundamental choice in my life. I have been learning, studying and searching for answers to difficult questions, with a commitment to share what I discover. It has not always been easy. It is especially difficult when one attempts to share the truth with those who are not ready to hear the truth. Remember Jack Nicholson's famous line in **A Few Good Men?** *"You want the truth? The truth? You can't handle the truth."* Many of us can't.

The big choices in your life guide your day-to-day

choices. They set the goals and even the agenda for most of what you do on a daily basis. As an example, you need to spend this morning working on a business plan for growing your practice because you have chosen wealth, and wealth requires that you continue to grow your practice. It is important for you to understand the simple, yet powerful idea that without fundamental choices you will not have a compass or sense of direction in your personal or business life.

I talk with far too many confused people. Because they are confused, their lives get complicated. The more complicated their lives get, the more they lose time and energy. It isn't long before they are trapped in the very structure they have created. Life becomes a *"path of least resistance"*; only it's a life that is going nowhere. It's going nowhere because the structures present in this life are guided by this "path of least resistance": Living day-to-day, week-to-week, and month-to-month; but with no thought of how each day creates the future.

When I talk with these people, they can't tell me what they want out of life. All they can tell me is that their lives are full of problems. These people are unclear and unsure about the direction they should take to remedy their problems. They know they want and are searching for something different in life, but they have no vision of what they want to create or how to even begin to change their circumstances. They are not creating a life of abundance and wealth because they don't even recognize they need to do so. They are simply mired in problem-solving. Because problem-solving without creative thinking breeds negativity, they become overwhelmed in the "details" of life. They are unable to focus upon the larger picture.

We all know people like this. It isn't long before they lose momentum and energy and find that they can't focus on doing the right work. If you don't know what you want and don't want it badly enough, you'll never put in the effort to find the way to create it.

People who don't know what they want spend their entire lives reacting to what they have. They know of no other way but reacting. A business or practice run in a reactionary mode leads to a life spent in reacting not creating. This is the main reason why 90% of all professionals and small business owners never create significant wealth in their lives. Generally, a life spent reacting to business and personal problems leads to a life spent reacting to money problems. Wealth is not the by-product of reacting to money problems. Reacting to money is a one-way ticket to nowhere.

Understand that people make fundamental choices for very different reasons. Your reasons for choosing wealth may differ significantly from mine. That's why I stress the exercise of making a list of all the important payoffs you believe will come to you as a result of creating wealth. Your choice to pursue wealth is also a choice to seek those payoffs.

Let's focus on that list of payoffs right now. Make your list of all the payoffs you think will come to you as a result of creating wealth in your life. Feel free to add to this list and continue to think about what's on this list. Here's what I want you to focus on. If what's on the list are things of primary importance to you, then you will find the knowledge and energy, the strategies and the actions, to create wealth. If the payoffs on the list are few and are not of primary importance to you, you will probably not be able to create significant wealth in your lifetime.

I believe this is one of the primary lessons I've learned these past years and why I am emphasizing this. Many people are simply not honest with themselves or with others about money and wealth issues. This is a very dangerous situation. I will write more about this in a later chapter.

Let me finish with a few words about choosing to create something. Creative choices are very powerful. The act of creating something also brings out the creator in you. Creating lifts your spirit. Problem-solving, by comparison, is just trying to fix something that is broken. That is necessary sometimes; but, when it dominates your life it can only take you through endless cycles of pain, struggle and negativity.

When you are creating, you are hopeful and positive about your future. You believe you will find innovative ways to create what you want. Creative people are happy people because they are engaged in creating a better life for themselves, their family, and others. When you think about it, you see that creative people accomplish so much more than those who sit by idly and watch the creators.

Choosing to create wealth is, for most of us, key to enjoying our life. At first, you may find the process of creating wealth confusing and disorienting. Don't worry, this is normal. It takes everyone some time to adjust to new ways. Persevere, as they used to tell the people in wagon trains setting out to build new lives on the frontier. Persevere and in a short time you will discover that you have developed the habits which will create wealth in your life and business. It is no more complicated than that.

In the next chapter I will write about what happens to a professional who does not know how to build wealth. ■

The Science of Creating Wealth™

This isn't an unusual story. The man I'm going to talk to you about is not unrepresentative of thousands of professionals whom I've met these past 35 years. His story certainly isn't meant as a criticism or an indictment of anyone. I don't believe that he or most people are bad or evil or stupid. Quite the contrary, I believe most people are good, well intentioned and intelligent.

The story represents all that is wrong about our educational system and our professional training. I really want to share it with you. I will use the name "John", but the story could be about "Judy". Better than 50% of all professionals today are women.

John graduates from professional school, takes his residency in an area of professional practice, and associates with a firm or practice for a period of time, all the while learning the ropes of dentistry. John eventually decides he wants to have more autonomy, more freedom, and a better chance to run his own show. He decides he will either start a practice or buy one. He takes the leap. Still in debt from school and now more in debt, John opens his office with a great deal of hope and excitement.

John's first goal is to be busy. He needs to be busy because he has a great deal of debt, not to mention rent, salaries, and general operating expenses to cover. In time, because John has a pleasing personality and is enjoyable to be around, he does get busy. The busier John gets, the more successful he thinks he has become. Because he works hard, he feels he's earned the right to reward himself with a few things for his efforts. He buys a new car and runs that through his business. On the recommendation of his accountant, he joins a country club to meet people and deducts those fees from his tax bill.

Over the next ten years or so, John moves into a nicer home and begins to buy more "toys", including several expensive collector cars. He is able to lease and write off many of these things through his business. John is building an affluent lifestyle for himself.

It's a familiar story, right? The professional gets into a cozy relationship with his accountant, and a pattern develops. The pattern seems innocent enough, but there is a real potential for abuse. In the name of tax avoidance, John is encouraged to buy things and run them through his business. Well, why shouldn't he try to reduce his tax burden? That's not the point. Instead of saving and investing, finding creative people who know ethical, creative ways to optimize John's tax deductible pension contributions, John is encouraged to consume. And he is consuming far too much, abetted by a structure with money that facilitates, if not encourages, over-consumption, increases in taxes, personal spending and leaves John tied to the dental chair!

After 20 years of this, John, now 45, has taken in nearly $20 million in gross revenues. He has built a comfortable lifestyle for himself, but has created little or no wealth. The costs of his pattern of overconsuming now come home to roost. John's three kids are nearing college age. He has managed to fund only token college savings plans, so the costs of their education must now start coming out of ordinary business income. This puts a lot of pressure on him to produce more. He also has his own ever-escalating living expenses to cover. He can't just cancel the usual summer Mediterranean cruise, can he? What would his friends think? He needs to produce more. In his practice, labor costs are rising sharply. He needs to produce more. Everywhere John's costs are going up and the only way he has to offset them is to produce more. The pressure on him becomes tremendous.

John and his obliging accountant have unwittingly prepared a train wreck. The assumption they both made was that John could boundlessly increase his revenues to meet his expenses. It was not necessary to save and invest and forego some toys, because John could always increase his production to pay for whatever came up. The train could always go faster and faster. But they forgot something important. In the real world, trains can't keep going faster and faster, and when they go too fast, they derail. The structure of John's life, the unconscious structures that John and his willing accountant have crafted have and will continue to produce the "'path of least resistance" that John experiences. Unless he changes his fundamental choices and his underlying structure, John, like hundreds of thousands like him, will be "tied to the chair" and never be able to retire with dignity. Worse, John, his wife and family and all those he impacts, including his staff and clients, will never get John's best. In a professional life of reaction, John will never truly reach his God-given potential.

I told you John's story was not an unusual one. I bet most of you know a "John" or a "Judy". How do intelligent, well-intentioned people get themselves into these traps? John and his accountant allowed a bad pattern to evolve in his life and business. Maybe we should pause for a few minutes and think about bad patterns and how they come to be.

One thing I've noticed is that many professionals have a tendency to allow their businesses to grow, not by design or plan, but by default. Unplanned growth is not a good idea. Unplanned growth means the business develops along a "path of least resistance". Unplanned growth is caused by structure, just as planned growth is caused by structure. One structure leads to chaos and one leads to order. Unplanned growth spawns and nurtures bad patterns.

The following three patterns of unplanned growth, unfortunately, are very common.

- **Pattern 1.** The main focus becomes higher production and rapidly growing the business. More and bigger are assumed to be better.

The values of the owner and organization are buried or lost in the pursuit of production to feed the overhead of the growing machine. The business becomes a quick-fix, problem-solving machine with little attention paid to the true values of the owner or the business. The result is a big money chasing operation with its focus totally on growing production to keep up with ever increasing expenses. Production and consumption do not equal wealth!

- **Pattern 2.** The business becomes a cash cow to feed the owner's lifestyle. The focus is not on professional excellence or the creation of wealth and value for clients, but on supporting the lifestyle of the owner or owners. The more the owner(s) become addicted to a lavish lifestyle, the more the business is pressed to create the revenue to sustain the lifestyle for the owner. The business produces a lot of money but fails to create enduring, stable wealth. (I could call this "John's Model".)

- **Pattern 3.** The business is both production-oriented and lifestyle-oriented. The business is pushed to get bigger, to produce more, and to feed more into the owners' lifestyles. The focus of the business is intensely inward-looking and topline. The creation of value for customers, patients, or clients is an outward-looking value that does not register on this company's radar.

Each of these patterns, I think you can see, is a recipe for professional and financial disaster. How a business run in any of these ways that mistreats its clients is a topic for another time. What we are talking about now is the financial disaster they are preparing by failing to create wealth. Wealth is not created by unplanned growth.

What is the magnitude of the financial disaster these patterns are courting? Let me share a frightening statistic with you. Different professions vary, but on average, in my profession, by the age of 55, a dentist has saved about $255,000 for the future. Isn't that amazing? Think about the purchasing power of $255,000. Think about trying to retire on $255,000. You will not be living on easy street to say the least!

An average of $255,000 saved for retirement is proof that John's story is not unrepresentative. He was a well-intentioned, bright, professionally competent person who just did not know anything about **The Science of Creating Wealth™**. That ignorance cost dearly in his middle and later years. We don't want to let this happen to us.

"Without a vision, the people perish." That quote is not from **Exodus,** but it explains in a few words the 40 years the Israelites spent wandering in the desert after escaping

Pharaoh. They had solved the *problem* of their captivity in Egypt, but they had, as yet, no vision of their *future* – no vision of where they were going and of what nation they would establish. Forty years is a long time to wander around in the wilderness. You and I don't have forty years to wander around not knowing what kind of life we want to create.

John had no vision of the life he really needed to create for himself. He overspent on "toys" and other signs of affluence, never looking into the future. John thought problem solving and reacting to whatever came up was enough. His catechism and rule book for living were the tax code and standard accounting practices. Sadly, there is nothing in either that is proactive or forward-looking. Accounting is not a science for creating wealth. It never was and never will be as long as traditional accounting methods are used to keep score.

I think I'm on safe ground when I say this. You are either busy creating the life you want or busy reacting to your life you have. Does that make sense to you? When you look back at your own life, from before you started your own business right up to the present, can you see any recurring bad patterns of behavior with money? Can you see yourself in any of the patterns I have described?

Please take time right now and write down what you believe your patterns are or have been. This is an important exercise. Do it now.

I'd like to share an experience I had with a long time friend and client. I'll explain afterwards why I'm telling you this story.

In 1970, my attorney, Elliot Simon, gave me a book entitled, **The Richest Man in Babylon.** He told me in no uncertain terms to read it, and if I didn't want to live by its principles, he didn't want me as a client!

Jump forward four years to 1974, I was lecturing about this book to a small in-house group at the Pankey Institute. Among those in the room was my friend and eventual client, Dr. Bob. Jump ahead another 15 years (to 1989) and I was lecturing in Orlando, Florida. Dr. Bob was again in the audience. Again, the topic was creating wealth and abundance. Below is the note Bob wrote to me after the lecture:

> *"You remember, don't you, that I listened to your Pankey presentation in 1974? Today, after hearing your presentation for the second time, I have decided to join you. I quote from one of our favorite sources,* **The Richest Man in Babylon:**
>
> *'Die in the desert! Not I!*
> *With a new vision (picture), I saw the thing*
> *I must do. Where there is determination (will),*
> *the way can be found.'*
>
> *Thanks for your guidance. — Dr. Bob M."*

Why am I telling you this story? I'm sharing it with you because at any time any person can decide to program their brain in ways that will create wealth. The combination of your intellect, your emotions, and your will power always determines what you get. Notice the reference to dying in the desert. The earlier you stop wandering around in the desert, the earlier you can step out of the patterns of behavior you are trapped in and begin to create wealth, abundance and freedom in your life. Dr. Bob got it, but not at first exposure. In fact, it took him 15 years to get it.

Any time you want, you can choose to save rather than spend. You can invest in appreciating assets rather than throwing your money away. You can take responsibility for your money rather than letting others control it. You can forego or delay instant gratifications rather than impulsively spend everything you make.

I assume you are reading this book because you are part of the silent majority of professionals. You are well trained, you have strong professional skills, and you probably have a family and many other responsibilities. You keep asking yourself, *"how can I create wealth?"* No answer comes to mind. I'm saying to you, there is an answer and it is surprisingly simple.

At any time you choose, you can break away from your current financial patterns and create new ones. You can replace what hasn't worked with what will work. With a new vision of your business, you will begin to see what you must do.

You can make the choice to change today or wait another 15 years. I recommend that you do it today, but that's your choice. No one can make it for you, and you will not make it until you understand why you need to create wealth in your life.

Remember at the beginning of Chapter Three, we discussed this principle: ***"Structure determines patterns of behavior determine results"***. Well, in time our patterns of behavior become ingrained habits. Habits are important because much of our behavior is habitual at the unconscious level.

Here's a recent story I'd like to share. A former staff member and patient of mine was diagnosed with terminal cancer. It had invaded every major organ of his body. This was one of the most intelligent people I have ever known. He was one of the originators of the Lotus spreadsheet. My friend and patient unfortunately had two bad habits. He drank whiskey and a lot of it, and he never could quit smoking.

Some people would say he was the victim of bad luck. He lost the cancer lottery that kills more than a quarter of us. I don't think bad luck is the major culprit here. I think my friend created or helped create exactly what he got. It is my belief that he gave himself cancer with his two bad habits. What I've seen many times is this: Bad habits create bad luck, good habits create good luck.

What I didn't emphasize earlier, as we surveyed the bad financial habits of John and others, is that bad habits or patterns can be replaced by good habits. Habits are not permanent nor unchangeable. The keys to change are motivation (desire), awareness, knowledge, and practice. If you want to change, know what changes you need to make, and how to make them, then you will make them. Bad habits are not only problems to be overcome; they are opportunities to create new and better habits.

Bad habits and patterns cause us to make mistakes. We all make mistakes. Life is a series of opportunities to make choices and learn from ones that didn't work. But sometimes we don't learn. We repeat the same mistakes over and over, as if we couldn't learn from them or change our behavior. This is a bad pattern. You can learn and you can change, believe me.

Sometimes it helps to look at the lives of successful people (success defined simply as creating what you want) and see how they've learned from their mistakes. I'm going to predict something that will occur to you as you look at successful people. What separates the successful from those who aren't is that successful people have a vision of what they want to create. They have a vision and are constantly reminding themselves of it. They become creators rather than reactors and victims of life.

Bad habits and patterns, I said, cause us to make mistakes. When we become too busy and drop the habit of reflecting on our life, we open the door to all sorts of mistakes. It is critically important to regularly examine and reflect upon our lives. The first step is to reserve a weekend several times a year as a retreat. Devote that weekend to examining your past and your current behavior, and do this as honestly as you can. One of the things that will happen is that you will start to recognize the important people, events, and actions that are shaping your life. Who is most influential in your life? How are they affecting your behavior? Who or what is shaping your thinking? Look for patterns in your thinking and behavior.

By examining our lives we uncover the patterns of behavior that are shaping our lives and our future – unless we resolve to change. A new client to my Business Development Program shared this story with me.

> "After a certain time, I found myself following the same pattern that my dad did. My dad is a dentist and he's 65 now and can't afford to retire. There are many things I love about my dad, but I don't want to be where he is when I'm his age."

Like Scrooge in **The Christmas Story,** not until he had seen his past, present, and future was this client motivated to create something different. We all need to pause and reflect on our life, our business, and even our relationships. What patterns control our behavior in each of these arenas? If you think you are too busy to do this, then you are someone most in need of it. If you don't have the money to join a community that is devoted to creativity and accountability in life, then you probably won't get the guidance you need to achieve your personal goals.

I've lost my way before. I got off the path to a healthy life, but I will never do it again. I've even gotten off my path to creating wealth, but I will never do that again. We are all human. We are not perfect. We make mistakes. The question is not whether we make mistakes, but whether we helplessly continue to make the same mistakes over and over again. ■

The Science of Creating Wealth™

CHAPTER 7

Have a Positive View of Money

*"Mind is the Master Power that molds and
makes. And we are mind. And ever more
we take the tool of thought, and shaping
what we will, bring forth a thousand joys,
or a thousand ills. We think in secret,
and it comes to pass, environment,
is but our looking glass.* — James Allen

You are busy either creating what you want or reacting to what you have. It's that simple. Once you start reacting, it becomes a pattern created by the underlying structures that you will use every day – in your relationships, in your business and in every other part of your life. You and your business become a reaction to what is going on in your world. Do you want that?

The alternative is to become a creator of what you truly want in your life. Once you become a creator, it is easier to continue to create. There is an old adage, *"nothing succeeds like success"*. I prefer to say, *"nothing succeeds like creating"*.

Creating is the missing element or strategy in the systems most people have. In building a life devoted to problem-solving and reacting, they fail to create the things which are important to them. Is wealth important to you? Do you want wealth in your life? Let's talk about how you create it.

I'm going to focus on two keys to creating wealth. The first is to **(1) create a positive view of money.** Negative concepts or beliefs about money jam the positive creative process. Then you must **(2) create a plan of what it will take to create wealth.** Your life is waiting for you to create your life plan. You might think that creating a positive view of money is an unnecessary or superfluous step, but it isn't. Let me explain why.

A positive view of money does not come naturally to everyone. My father was a great thinker and a tremendous intellect. He had intelligence, will power and character. But he had a fixed idea about money that never changed throughout his life, and as a result, he died a rather poor man. He subscribed to the old view that money is the root of all evil.

The reason I know this is because he shared his thoughts on money with me many times. He told me that his father had inherited great wealth. Something over $20M in 1930, a huge sum in depression-era dollars. My dad's father divorced my grandmother in 1940 and she received a $4M settlement. In my dad's opinion, it was the wealth in the family that caused the divorce. He never changed his mind about this. Money was to blame for breaking up the family. Though he was brilliant in other areas, he would never turn his mind toward any kind of wealth creation. He thought to avoid wealth rather than create it.

My father thought he found justification for his animus

toward money in the Bible. He would quote *"Money is the root of all evil."* as if it were scripture. Actually, the passage in Timothy 6:10 says *"For the love of money is the root of all evil."* That is something different. What the Bible is condemning is the emotion of greed, which puts money-making above everything else and values only money.

Neither loving money nor hating it is a good idea. The greedy man and the man like my father who despises money both limit and handicap themselves with their prejudices. Creating wealth is not about falling in love with or worshipping money. It is about learning to use money to design the life you desire.

We are all limited by our beliefs, especially those which tell us something is good or bad. Money is such an emotional issue that few of us are without some biases on the subject. Be aware that your beliefs and feelings complicate what should be a fairly straightforward process of creating wealth in your own life. My father's beliefs made it completely impossible for him to create wealth despite his intelligence. Negative beliefs about money and wealth can undermine and sabotage everything you do to create wealth.

Maybe you are already aware of this. Our thoughts, positive or negative, are an extremely powerful creative force in our life. What you think about, you will ultimately create. Wealth or scarcity, health or illness, success or failure – so be careful what you think!

This is what I love about the Creative Process. Once

you learn to create, you start using your mind in ways you've probably never used it. You use it in a way that is more powerful than ever. Even if you've spent years working to improve your performance in business and life. This how we were designed. We, you and I, were designed to create.

There is no other process that is as useful and powerful as the Creative Process. In time, you will become a more powerful instrument in the creation of your business and life.

You may not be ready to accept what I am going to tell you now, but listen to it. *Whatever you have in your life at this moment – the quality of your relationships – your ability to create significant value in the lives of those for whom you care, or serve – the state of your own health – your knowledge, skills and abilities – your ability to organize your skills into useful, powerful forms of action – the amount of financial wealth (abundance) you have – the love you share with your spouse and children and family – you have created!* That's right – you are **100% responsible** and accountable for whatever you have (or lack) in your life right now.

You are 100% responsible for the life and business you have created, and you will be 100% responsible for the life and business you create in the future. I say this as much to myself as I say it to you. I, Michael Schuster, am 100% responsible for the life and business I have created and I will be 100% responsible for the life and business I will create in my future.

One of the reasons I continue to read Allen's **As a Man**

Thinketh, is that he reminds me that a single idle thought does materialize into a creation. And, when ideas are repeated often enough, be aware and beware, they become the seeds of the Creative Process. Whatever you continue to focus upon, Senge explains, will become an inner "Path of Least Resistance". Your energy will follow that path and what you are focused upon will lead to that creation.

Clarity about what you want is vitally important. If you are not clear about what you want, then that is the first step. **Get clear! It is worth any price to know what you want in life**. Lee Iacocca stated this several years ago. *"The first job of a salesperson is to help the client know what he or she wants. The second is to bust your tail to help them get it."* In the business of creating the life you want, you are both the salesman and the client. Do a good job selling yourself in your life. You are the architect and the contractor of your life. You design it and then execute it!

Creating, all true creating, comes from the inside out. Clarify your inner picture and then you have something to take into the world and build. It was Ted Turner who wrote about what most call Vision and what some of us call the Future Picture. *"A visionary is supposed to have a vision of the future"*, said Ted. We should all be visionaries.

As you are creating and clarifying your inner picture of what you want, there is one other thing I want you to keep in mind. As my friend Chuck Hogan likes to say, *"You can have **anything** you want, but you can't have **everything** you want."*

While creating tension between the Future Picture and present reality is a constructive thing to do, you can also create conflict within yourself. You want one thing and you also want another thing, but you begin to see that it is impossible to have both of these things at the same time. Conflicting financial goals might be a continued high rate of savings in the next year and also a major capital expansion with significant upfront outlays. Accept that these are conflicting goals and choose which is more important. Conflicting desires will only create inner gridlock and lead to no advancement.

On the other hand, re-enforcing or co-operating goals help the Future Picture reach fruition. Success breeds success. Successfully realizing one piece of the Future Picture leads to success with another, especially if the goals are properly sequenced. Here's an example from the Wealth Creation System (WCS) I invented 30 years ago.

The WCS is so structured that implementing one structure – I call them Advancing Structures – enables the next. I create one system that leads to better control of cash flow, and this creates a significant rise in net profit. This in turn, funds the creation of a more effective and efficient delivery of care and services. This leads to dramatically increased effectiveness in sales. This mandates an increase in production to keep pace with sales. This leads to a dramatic increase in net profits, which feed back into better sales and delivery. The total structure has what engineers call "high synergy". The bottom line for you is more time and money to create the life you want, and a realistic goal of financial independence in a 10-12 year horizon. The formula, as we will see, is a proper balance of net profit, tax reduction, tax-deferred pension planning, and personal lifestyle expenses.

Next, I want to write about setting goals on the path to wealth.

The Science of Creating Wealth™

CHAPTER 8 ■

Outcomes

The key is to know what you want and put your mind to creating it. Some people have stronger desires than others. I have come to understand this, though I believe that each person was put here for a purpose and has a gift to give to the world.

Traditional education does not help us discover our purpose or our gift. I can't write this book without invoking one of the most powerful messages I have ever read. I have to share this with you because I believe modern psychology has moved far away from its original intentions. In my view, it has become something different than it was intended to be; and not something better.

The perspective I want to offer is that psychology should not be another useless science. Psychology should actually help us understand ourselves and live our lives to get the things we want. Does that make sense to you?

It seems to me that all psychological systems can be divided into two types: First, we have those systems which study man as they find him, or as they suppose him to be. Modern scientific psychology belongs in this category. Second, we have systems which study man not from the point of view of what he is or what he seems to be, but from the point of view of what he may become. What he may become if we think of Homo sapiens' genome as something we might completely rewrite in the laboratory, or what he might become from the point of view of his current unmanipulated evolution.

The last kind of system is in reality the original one, or in any case, the oldest one. These systems attempt to explain the forgotten origin and meaning of psychology. That origin, I believe, was the idea that man, as we know him, is not a completed being. Nature guides or controls his development only up to a certain point. Then it's up to the individual. He can choose to develop further, by his own efforts and devices, or he can choose to stagnate and degenerate. Development in this case means primarily the emergence of certain inner qualities and features, which otherwise would remain undeveloped. These qualities cannot develop spontaneously. Experience and observation have shown that their development is possible only under certain favorable conditions – through specific efforts on the part of the individual himself, and with sufficient help from those who have previously done similar work and have already attained a certain level of development, or, at least, certain knowledge of the appropriate methods.

We must start with the idea that without motivation and effort, self-directed individual development is impossible. Without help, it is also impossible. The development of the individual depends upon his understanding of what he may obtain by it and what he must give for it. If a man does not

The Science of Creating Wealth™

want to develop in this way, or if he doesn't want it enough to make the necessary efforts, he simply will not develop. It is not an injustice that not everyone grows in this way. Ask yourself this question, *"Why should a man get what he doesn't want?'*

The key to individual development is learning to use the Creative Process. As I suggested earlier, once you engage in any truly Creative Process, you develop and grow. You learn to pursue what you want to create. Your second creation will be better than your first. Your third better than your second and so it goes. You learn, you develop, you become more as you create more.

For myself and for those with whom I have been privileged to work, it has been a joy to see their lives become far more fun, creative, alive, and complete. The transition from a problem-solving orientation to a creative orientation has been the most fruitful strategy I learned in my own life. It has also been the most useful strategy or process I've taught to my patients and clients over these past several decades.

If I am going to write about individual development and the Creative Process, I need to revisit a topic I wrote about in Chapter Five and pay my first visit to a new topic. Fundamental choices and goals are topics I want to talk about to you.

Remember the list of fundamental choices or commit-ments I shared with you in Chapter Five? Here is a similar list:

HEALTH   WEALTH   TRUTH
BEAUTY   LONGEVITY

What I want you to think about now is how all five of these fundamental choices could be structured to support one another and aid in mutual advancement. Think, for example, about wealth and contribution. I find it difficult to comprehend how anyone or any business can create wealth without making a significant contribution to their patients or clients. The greater the value created in this way, the greater the potential for creation of wealth. Some people like to talk about "giving back" as a way to create wealth. "Giving back" is the same thing as contribution.

Think about wealth and health. First of all, can a person think creatively about something that they have not chosen for themselves? I doubt it. So when someone is unhealthy and hasn't chosen to create health in their own life, how can that person help other people create health? Similarly, how can someone help others create wealth, when they have not chosen to create wealth for themselves? And how can someone who has chosen neither health nor wealth understand or teach another the synergy of creating health plus wealth? Certain fundamental choices strongly support one another, but only people who have chosen to develop them in tandem in their own lives know this.

It would be wrong to say that someone who hasn't made a fundamental choice to create health and wealth and truth in his life doesn't know what he wants. Other choices are possible and valid. But in my experience, almost everyone who hasn't made these big choices doesn't know what he wants or at least has no idea about how to get what he wants. This brings us to the topic of the necessity of establishing clear, well-defined goals and objectives.

Manifest your desires into your intentions and your intentions into your creations. That's very good advice. Exchange these two words: "Goals" for "Intentions", and you know exactly where I am going. Anyone who doesn't know what they want and can't or won't establish clear goals and objectives will find it difficult, if not impossible, to succeed. The other side of the coin is also true. Anyone who knows what he wants and has a very clear intention (goal) to create it will soon find the conditions to support his vision.

"When the student is ready, the teacher will appear." Think about being ready and committed to creating wealth in your life. The getting ready point occurs when you decide to set goals. Most of us need some help and advice in setting our goals. Goal setting is a real art. At the point we are ready, the book, the seminar, the teacher, the guide, the coach, or the mentor always, and I mean always, appears. It never fails.

The most successful people I have met, and I've met plenty of them, have set one predominate goal or aspiration in their life. One dominant aspiration drives their life, and it is always about creating something. For me, it has been the pursuit of knowledge and learning; but not just for its own sake. Knowledge should be shared and taught for the betterment of everyone.

Can you identify one dominant aspiration in your life? What is it? Some of you will say it is to become the best human being you can be physically, mentally, emotionally and spiritually. That's very good, but is it enough?

I always wanted to share what I learned with others. Sharing benefits others' lives and mine. This book is part of that mission. There has always been so much misinformation and deception in the marketplace of ideas. When I gain new knowledge and successfully apply it, I want to share that new experience with as many who will listen.

Goals are your commitment to what you want to achieve or become. With goals you can create your future. Without goals you will simply continue to relive your past. When you set a goal or an end result, you automatically begin to program your mind to seek the answers (actions or strategies) needed to achieve that end result. In a favorite book of mine, **Psychocybernetics,** the author, Maxwell Maltz, writes, *"The mind is a cybernetic (self-directing), teleological (being directed towards a definite purpose) organism and it works like this. If you don't know the goal or end result, all of your energy is channeled to find the goal. Once the goal is known, then the mind works in a creative fashion to discover how to achieve the goal."*

I've devoted a lifetime of study to the great creators. I've even been able to work with some of them in the real world. What I have discovered is that these extremely creative people are not like average folks. They are more like Maslow's self-actualizers. Maslow wrote, *"Self-actualized people see life clearly. They are objective, and thus, are less likely to allow*

The Science of Creating Wealth™

hopes, fears, or defenses to distort their perceptions of reality. They are committed to something greater than themselves and able to do well at their chosen goals. They work hard and are spontaneous and creative and courageous in their everyday lives."

According to Maslow, self-actualizers are relatively free of neuroses and make excellent use of their talents and develop more of their innate potential. However, they are not perfect. In his final book, Maslow describes eight kinds of habits or behavioral patterns which lead to self-actualization. These eight behaviors are so important to becoming a highly creative person that I'm going to take you through them one by one.

The self-actualizer **concentrates.** Maslow says, "Self-actualization means experiencing fully, vividly, selflessly. It is the capacity to see the actual situation occurring now and in the present and seeing it clearly. It is seeing with as few personal filters, beliefs, concepts and agenda as possible."

The self-actualizer **chooses growth.** Maslow writes, "Life is a series of choices. We can choose to be safe, to hang back, to do what has been done before. On the other hand, we can choose to innovate and grow, to challenge and to be challenged, to be stretched to learn. Being safe carries the risk of regressing and shrinking back into our former selves. To choose growth is to choose to remain open, to be bold enough to look forward to the unknown."

The self-actualizer **has self-awareness.** He writes, "Self-actualizing rests on becoming more aware of our own inner nature and acting in accord with it. This means to be able to decide for myself what I want to do, what I like, and what are my genuine needs. It is the result of heightened ability to be able to discriminate between external manipulation by others, by culture, by society and internal realities."

The self-actualizer is **honest.** Maslow says, "Each time we are honest and take responsibility for our own action, we move toward greater self-actualization. Posturing or giving answers to please others lowers the ability to self-actualize and create. Self-actualizers love the truth, even when it is unflattering or disturbing. They see the power that telling the truth gives them in their lives."

The self-actualizer trusts his own **judgment.** He writes, "Self-actualizers learn to respect and trust their own judgments and their own instincts." Maslow adds that this trust leads to choices that are right for the individual.

The self-actualizer is committed to **self-development.** "Self-actualization is the process of developing our potentialities. It is to work well, and do the work we want to do. We may have great talent, but unless we develop that talent, we are not self-actualizing. The process of self-actualizing is ongoing (just as the process of creating is ongoing). It is the never-ending process of making real our potentials, continually living, working, and relating to the whole; not only to a single accomplishment or even a series of accomplishments."

The self-actualizer seeks **peak experiences.** Maslow says, "Peak experiences are those transient moments of self-

actualization. These are times when we think, feel and act most clearly and accurately. We are more loving, more accepting of others, temporarily free of inner conflicts and anxiety. We are better able to put our energies to creative use."

The self-actualizer has let down his **defenses.** *"When we see and recognize our own beliefs, concepts, defenses and negative habit patterns, and let them go, we can act in healthier, more creative ways. One way is to become more aware of the various ways we obscure our self image and thus, distort the view of the outer world."*

Each of these characteristics which Maslow identified in the healthiest and highest performing individuals provide important clues about how we can change from being reactive, problem-solving individuals to true self-actualizers. The habitual ways we have been trained to think and act don't serve us. The art and science of creating is the opposite of reactive methods of living and conducting our business.

I want to now write about an important distinction between goals. Some goals are tangible, others intangible. Tangible goals include things like higher production or net profit, better cash flow, and less debt. Tangible goals also include acquiring more assets such as homes, boats, planes, and horses. Intangible goals are things like better health and relationships, more skills and leisure, inner peace and contentment.

The pursuit of tangible goals can aid and support achieving intangible goals. For example, longer life expectancy in the United States is directly related to higher income. Being well off financially does not always improve your health, but it does enable you to get better quality medical care, which means you have a good chance of recovering from illnesses that could be fatal. We live in a material world. Life is much easier if you have sufficient financial resources to cover your needs.

This is a classic statement from James Fadiman. *"Learning to achieve greater material success has proven to be easy, obvious and effective."*

The Science of Creating Wealth™ is predictable, reliable, and without error. Surprisingly, results have shown that it is not difficult to teach people to have enough money. Studies of hundreds have shown that the goal of economic security (financial independence) is actually an entrance goal, a gate which opens to reveal the goals beyond it.

Once people overcome their fears of not having enough money, they begin to work earnestly on improving their health and relationships. They remember the goal of personal satisfaction.

If you read Fadiman's statement several times, you begin to sense the power implicit in **The Science of Creating Wealth™**. It is absolutely essential for all of us to establish structures and put systems in place that allow us to create financial independence. Even those born to wealth need systems to protect and preserve their estates. The earlier you can achieve this, the earlier you can be free to create the life you want to live.

I don't think I need explain how wealth is supportive of other intangible goals such as relationships, friends, colleagues, and family. While it takes time to create wealth, those who have created wealth are able to enjoy significant quality time with their family and friends, free from chronic financial anxieties.

Some other intangible goals have to do with learning new ways of thinking, strengthening one's character, learning to manage time and energy more effectively, and having more time for relaxation, rest, renewal and recovery. Wealth enables all of these pursuits; while scarcity makes all of them harder to pursue.

As you learn how to use the Creative Process, you will begin to ask yourself some very important questions: *"Is this goal or end result something I really want, or does someone else want it for me? Am I freely choosing to do what I'm doing right now? Do I really enjoy what I am doing? Is this goal or end result something truly important to me? Do I need to create this result in my life? Are my goals clear, concise, and consistent with each other, or is there conflict among them?"*

The most important thing I can share with you right now is this: It is essential for you to create goals in every major aspect of your life. In any area where your goals involve serious change, set time limits for yourself, but don't be confined to the time limit.

I like the concept of "stretch goals". Whatever the area – wealth, health or relationships – I know I can always do better. I want to make progress, but I do not fall into the trap of chasing perfection. Life is a continuous progress or it isn't. Life is never exactly as we hoped it would be. That's why I have to continue to re-invent myself and create something new and fun, challenging and contributing. ∎

The Science of Creating Wealth™

CHAPTER 9 ∎

The Key Elements

What are the key elements in **The Science of Creating Wealth**™? The first and more powerful element is YOU. You have the intellect, the emotion and the will to create wealth if you choose to. I keep reminding you that you have this choice and power. I suspect some of you still don't believe me. You think wealth is not an option in your case. You think scarcity is the permanent condition in your world. Martin Seligman wrote a book about that kind of pessimism and how it kills creativity and achievement. The title of his book is his recommendation for overcoming this sort of debilitating pessimism. The title is **Learned Optimism.** Read it sometime, especially if you are still wondering whether you can choose wealth. I tell you again. Yes, you can.

To create wealth you need to know how your mind works. Ask it the right questions and it will start working to create wealth for you. It's really that simple to turn on the Creative Process. The first question is, *"What do I want?"* But more precisely, ***"What do I really want for its own sake?"*** Most things I want because they will get me other things. They are steps on the path toward a higher goal. Try to isolate the things you feel you want for their own sake.

Now ask yourself, *"Why do I want these things?"* I could write about this subject endlessly. If you don't know why you want what you say you want, you're really just manipulating yourself. You will never create a true path to achieving what you want. I've discovered one of the major flaws in goal setting. Many people don't achieve the goals they set because they've not taken the time to become clear about the payoffs associated with achieving the goal. What are the payoffs associated with the things you want most to achieve?

Next ask yourself, *"How do I do it?"* We are now in the world of "how to's." Everyone wants to know the 5 steps to this or the 7 keys to that. They read, they listen, they buy the CD's, go to the seminars and listen to their favorite gurus. All the information in the world is useless, unless you know how to apply it in your life.

You will never create wealth, or for that matter, anything you want, unless you know the WHAT, the WHY and the HOW.

I have mentioned this book several times before but want to specifically mention it now. The title is **The Richest Man in Babylon.** It is arguably the single most important book ever written about money. On the mirror in my closet are posted the *"Seven Cures for a Lean Purse".* I've read them every day for the last 37 years. I will share them with you a little later.

I have lectured on the fundamental principles of creating wealth since 1974, and invented a business model for professional practices (actually, it works for any business) that enables professionals to create wealth in 144 months or less.

The Science of Creating Wealth™ begins with a target ratio of savings and investments commensurate with your current living expenses. This wealth ratio should be about 20. In other words, your savings and investments should total about 20-25 times what your current after-tax living costs are. The math is simple right, right? If you spend about $100,000 annually, you want to set your goal at $2M to 2.5M in savings and investments. If you've had extraordinary expenses this year, take a three-year average or adjust it in whatever way seems appropriate to you.

When you reach this goal, when you have saved and invested 20-25 times your current expenses, (cost of living expenses), you've reached financial independence by any standard system of financial planning. Using your current (or average) annual personal consumption expenses as the basis, multiply that number by 25 and write down the exact amount of wealth you need to reach this goal, and the date by which you intend to reach it. "Some day" is not a date.

The amount of savings and investments I need to reach financially independence is $_____(amount). I will reach this goal by _____(date).

Now list all the benefits or payoffs you believe will accrue to you from creating wealth in your life. Do it right now.

_____

_____

_____

_____

_____

_____

I've given you a few lines in this book in which to write, but please try to list at least a dozen or more reasons to create wealth in your life. Use another sheet of paper and take some time to come up with more reasons. It is important that you write down as many of these payoffs as possible; keep them with your vision statement of why you want to create wealth.

Don't ever get too far away from your list. Write your goal, the date and your payoffs where you will see them and read them every day of your life. I do this with my health, with my wealth goals, and with my relationship goals.

If you didn't do this, if you think this is all some childish game, then you've failed the first test of being committed to creating wealth in your life. Perhaps you aren't ready? Maybe this isn't the right time? Or, you have decided to wait for awhile (procrastination) – a few years. Remember John and where he ended up? If you aren't willing to do this simple exercise, it really makes no sense to go further and waste your energy. In fact, just put this book down. Because without a firm dollar amount in mind, and the clear list of the payoffs from achieving this goal, you probably won't begin. Or, if you should begin, you will stop at some early point of resistance and reverse your course. Why bother?... Who do think is in control of what you are doing? If you are waiting for someone else to do it for you, it's not going to happen. Each of us are the only ones that will change our own behaviors in life. Frankly, there is just no one else who can do if for you. You are your master of your own destiny. It's just that simple!

So, the first major element is YOU. What you want, why you want it, and how you plan to get it. The "how" is the easiest and simplest part. Once you have decided to create wealth, you won't have time for anything but realistic, useful information.

If you can believe all of the financial self-help gurus, there are at least a million ways to create wealth. A man on television the other night was promising a 40% per annum return from reselling distressed oceanfront real estate. I just needed to wire him $100,000 to get started! I know I don't have to tell you to be very careful with this kind of thing. Ever hear the old adage, *"There is NOTHING free in life?"* Well, it's the same principle with "GET-RICH-QUICK" schemes. They do not happen. Stay away from these "come-ons". Even being slightly attracted to these pitches shows you are still thinking impulsively and reactively about your money. Is saving and investing a problem for you? YOU need to sit down and prepare your mind. Start thinking creatively rather than reactively about your money. And, it is YOUR money!

The idea of creating wealth is a very powerful one. When you determine that you want to create wealth, a second major factor comes into play. You now need to ask yourself, *"What am I prepared to give to others to create wealth in my life? What am I giving to others to get what I want? This for that, or 'quid pro quo'*," as the Romans used to say.

This is a crucial idea and the majority of people totally miss it. They create businesses which are to serve only them. They fail to realize that creating wealth honestly means that you must create something of significant value for the people or organizations that you serve. Then, and only then, are they willing to pay you a fee commensurate with the value you are creating.

All the greatest entrepreneurs know this. The rest fall into the trap of thinking that the world was created for them. We see some of these arrogant "the world is my oyster" people every day on television. They were the CEO's of large corporations; but now they are on trial for defrauding investors and breaking dozens of laws. They've disgraced themselves, betrayed the trust of their investors and clients, and earned themselves a long vacation in a federal prison. Excellent examples, all of them, of how NOT to create wealth.

Let me recap the main point. In order to create wealth, you must understand what you have to give others, to get something in return. It is easy to overlook this in the desire to get busy and make money. It's a trap that some professionals fall into over time. In the beginning, they created their business or practice with the best intentions, but over time, they've allowed it to turn into something else. They find they are trying to control a production-based business (where the goal is to pay the bills of the business) or a lifestyle-based business (where the goal is to fund the needs and lifestyle of its owners).

The Science of Creating Wealth™

Neither of these business strategies creates wealth or abundance. They do, for a period of time, enhance the lifestyle of the owners, but eventually the owners realize they have to start over. They realize they've created a money-monster that is doing nothing in the long term to create wealth and abundance for them. In the Wealth Development model, I teach that there are **three basic principles** that serve as the foundation of the creation of all wealth.

(1) First, You Have To Learn To Earn Money. Yes, this is obvious, but the statement needs elaboration. How much do you need to make? At least enough to pay your bills at home and in the business, and enough to pay your taxes and save or invest for the goal of financial independence. The amount will vary depending on other factors as well. Debt and interest rates are important ones. We will explore this in more detail later.

(2) Learn How To Keep The Money You've Earned. How much you need to make will also depend on whether you have learned how to keep it. This is the second principle. Certainly the relationship between income and outgo is a critical factor. If you don't learn how to keep what you make, then you will try to get ahead by making more and more. You can't keep doing that; eventually you will just keep less and less. Keeping what you make is, in part, a matter of being tax smart. What I have seen too often is that those who focus on making it (production) don't pay much attention to keeping it and are not tax savvy. The IRS loves these people!

What we have researched and documented at The

Schuster Center, is that the average professional overspends about $2,400,000 in expenses in a 30-year business cycle. This is a business that is taking in revenues of $800,000 a year. This same business owner, because of a lack of proper tax planning, will also pay $1,200,000 more in taxes over this 30 year period than the tax code requires. That math should inspire you. Learning to keep what you earn requires an effective tax strategy. Without one, all you will do is pay more income tax and never create wealth.

(3) You Have To Invest It, Don't Lose It. The third principle. Don't lose it by consuming it or by speculating with it.

The fundamental choice of creating wealth imposes a money discipline. It is a discipline because it is natural to spend everything you make. It is "unnatural" to save and invest and pay attention to your costs and develop a tax strategy that favors you and not Uncle Sam. It is properly called a discipline because controlling the flow of money in this way is something you must learn to do, not something you do naturally.

Now, this is not always simple. Sometimes you have to research and explore and even invent a new, safe, and reliable way to grow your savings. Save enough so that the money which you have worked hard to earn, grows and compounds, rather than shrinks and disappears. Preserving your wealth is part of creating wealth.

Next, I want to write about three simple, but powerful rules for controlling your money and creating wealth. ■

CHAPTER 10

Three Rules for Creating Wealth

I'm going to assume after the last chapter that you have made the fundamental choice to create wealth, and you have decided to do so within the next ten to twelve years. You have set your target dollar goal. You know where you want to go. You have your Future Picture of what you want to create, complete with the price tag. Now all you need is a little help. The three rules I will discuss in this chapter will be a big help.

- **Rule #1. Learn To Create Value.**

The only and everlasting source of profit is the creation of value. Believe that. It is essential that you learn to think differently about the business or profession that you are in. You must think more deeply and profoundly about what your patients, clients, and prospects really want. Not what YOU want, but what THEY want. We spent some time exploring this principle in Chapter Nine. In order to get what you want, you must give others what they truly want. We also will be speaking about how you determine the exact amount of money you need in order to create wealth and financial freedom in your life. Then, you must determine how you will create enough value for your clients so that they will help you achieve your outcome.

You cannot assume anything here. You cannot assume because one client wants one thing all of your other prospects or clients will want the same thing. Also, you cannot assume that what's important to you is what your client or prospect values the most.

To create value for your client, you must know what the client is truly seeking. This is the single most important and most violated law of creating wealth.

Learn to think from the client's perspective, not your own. You have to break out of that traditional mindset. Don't assume you know what your client wants. Ask questions, many questions, until you are certain you understand what he wants. Think about it this way. Your client has created a Future Picture in his mind of exactly what he wants. Get a good look at that picture.

Your job as a business owner is to create a product or service that your clients want. Sometimes you must help your client or patient clarify in technicolor terms exactly what it is they want. You can then tailor and fine-tune your product. That is your job, too. Don't be reluctant to do these jobs. If you are, your ability to be a true creator of wealth will be limited. Your profits will be limited. Limited by your inability to fulfill the aspirations of your clients.

Focus your business on creating something others value. Keep asking yourself, *"What do they really want?"* If you decide they don't really know what they want, then a relationship cannot be started until they do. You client must know what your product or service will do for him. *People buy for their own reasons, for their own payoffs, not yours.* This might seem to turn effective sales into mind reading, but it doesn't, because you are able to ask questions and listen to the answer. People will tell you what they really want. Don't be shy. Ask them and listen.

I can't emphasize this too much. In the sales training I've done, I find that inexperienced sales people don't ask questions. Instead, they fill in any blanks with their own agenda and their own ideas about the situation. The customer or client doesn't buy. Why? Because he was not offered something HE valued.

The next rule is about getting serious about money. *If your relationship with money isn't a serious one, you will never develop the discipline to create wealth, no matter how much money you make.* A savings strategy is simple but it requires discipline. If saving isn't already a habit, then a lot of discipline may be needed to succeed. No one does what they don't naturally want to do unless they see that it serves a higher purpose. When creating wealth in your life becomes a primary choice in your life, you will do what you would not naturally do to achieve this outcome. If wealth and the freedom it brings are not primary choices in your life, then you will not develop the discipline to achieve these outcomes. It's that simple; yet that profound. You are the maker, the master, and the creator of your own life.

And so, the reason for Rule #2.

- **Rule #2. The Key to Creating Wealth is Following a Savings Strategy.**

For every $10 dollars you put in your purse, take out and use only nine. Your purse will start to fatten at once and feel good in your hand bringing satisfaction to your soul. More good advice. Any person, regardless of income, age, race or religion can begin to create wealth by saving a part of everything he earns. Here's some arithmetic.

Suppose you had a job where you made $50,000 per year for 30 years. If you saved 10% or $5,000 per year, you would have taken $150,000 out of your paycheck over the 30 years. But how much would you end up with after 30 years? The power of compounding at 10% over 30 years is a remarkable thing. The answer may surprise you. You would have saved $904,717 (check the number)! With another year of earnings you would have saved more than a million. You could now turn around and start drawing out $50,000 a year (or 5%) and still be adding to your principal. You would never run out of money.

Redo this example with your income and your time horizon. The idea is to picture and then commit to a specific end result. When you have a specific picture of what you want, you will take action. Financial independence is what you want, but the concept, by itself, is not something specific and personal enough to be your goal.

Let me give you a few other examples of what regular contributions plus compounding can do for you. Suppose now you can make monthly contributions over the time periods indicated.

Monthly Investment	Years	Earnings rate	Total Net Worth
$5,000	10 yrs	10%	$1,077,350
$5,000	12 yrs	10%	$1,447,023
$10,000	10 yrs	10%	$2,101,575
$10,000	12 yrs	10%	$2,829,213
$5,000	20 yrs	10%	$3,940,657
$10,000	20 yrs	10%	$7,737,502
$20,883	7 yrs	10%	$2,565,213
$25,000	7 yrs	10%	$3,063,165

Or suppose you start at age 60 with $300,000 per year and make these monthly contributions:

$20,883	5 yrs	10%	$1,649,407
$20,833	7 yrs	10%	$2,565,213

It is obvious that starting early has the advantage of the long compounding period, but there are very good (tax deferred) plans that enable any professional, age 55-65, to create wealth in a short period of time.

I can already hear your next question. Where is this money for savings going to come from? First, it can come from excess overhead. My company's research and data for the past 30 years proves that ANYONE using the money strategies we created can increase their net profits by 10-12% of gross revenues by switching to our financial structure. It's just that simple! If you follow our business model, a $700,000 per year professional business can recapture $70,000-$84,000 in excess business spending. We also cut your tax burden and save you another $10,000-$30,000 a year. With just these two changes a $700,000 practice could reclaim $90,000 to $114,000 a year in earned dollars. This is money you can and should use to create wealth. You could invest all of these dollars in tax-reducing pension plans that target the creation of wealth in a 7-8 year time frame. Think about sound money management and tax reduction as tandem strategies for creating wealth.

Obviously, if you start late, you will have to play some catch up. But, if you have the end dollar result in mind, you can still do it. Trust the arithmetic. You can do it.

- **Rule #3. Control Your Expenses.**

Now, I'll tell you a truth about men and women. Whenever your income grows, your expenses will as well, unless you protest to the contrary. Spend what you will, but always save 10%! In my observation, spending money comes naturally. Saving and investing money is the "unnatural" act; and therefore, requires discipline. If you have not accumulated wealth in your years in business it is simply because you have not instigated a wealth creating structure in your life. Any professional can learn and implement a wealth creating structure which will alter the flow of money in their business and life. Think of a river bed. The water flows wherever the structure of a riverbed guides its flow. Learning to live on 90% while saving 10% doesn't seem difficult in the abstract, but it requires structure and a series of actions that are not practiced by professionals who are not creating wealth in their lives. The purpose of these actions is to redirect the flow of money in and out of your business and life to create wealth.

The Science of Creating Wealth™

You've heard this before I'm sure, but this is critical. You need a plan for your money or it will find its own "path of least resistance", and you will spend everything you make. In fact, you need at least four separate plans for your money. You need a **business spending plan**, a **personal spending plan,** a **tax savings plan** and a **savings and investment plan.**

I recommend a plan that uses percentage budgeting. Keep in mind, if you use traditional accounting methods, which are aimed at depreciation and taxes, you will not be focused on the numbers that create wealth for you. Traditional accounting just balances assets and liabilities with nothing in the entire process oriented toward creating wealth. Traditional accounting does a good job for what it was designed to do, which is to show you where your money went after you spent it.

Let me remind you that there are two basic orientations in life and business. Reactive and creative. Most businesses run with a reactive orientation that responds to a problem or an event after it has happened. When you get your accounting statement, no matter how timely, it is about what has already happened. Once the books for any given month, quarter, or year are closed, there is simply nothing you can do about either what you produced, collected, or spent.

Percentage budgeting has a creative orientation. Percentage budgeting puts you in the drivers seat. A percentage budget is creative because it tells you, based on what you decided in advance, what you can and can't spend in each category of expenditure. You can even plan for tax consequences rather than having to cope, after the fact, with the tax consequences of what you've already made and spent.

You decide *in advance* how much you will spend in each of the major categories of expenditure. You decide *in advance* how much money you will save and invest every week, month, quarter and year. It is not necessary for you to put tight limits on all kinds of spending. The primary idea is that you decide in advance what amount is reasonable to spend in any area. Budgets are a very important part of the structure of creating wealth.

In conversations with accountants, attorneys, and financial planners, I find that many of them have a difficult time grasping how and why this works. I think I understand why. They have been taught in their professional life to be reactive, not creative.

In creating we decide in advance what we want. We determine a specific result we want and then look to create a path to that result based on where we are starting from. It is impossible to create from a reactive orientation which seeks only to escape a current problem.

There is a big difference between thinking about how to create a business that has the production, cash flow, overhead, taxes and net profits you want as opposed to thinking about how to fix a business with problems in these areas. Make this shift in thinking and you will see immediately how enjoyable working in the creative mode can be.

Percentage budgeting is a creative discipline that seeks

to predetermine where money will flow. Left to itself, money, just like water, doesn't know where to go. It begins to follow a "path of least resistance", which means that your spending is not only without controls but out of control. You can't build wealth when spending is out of control. That makes sense to you, doesn't it? Money that is not earmarked for something will be consumed, not saved or invested.

There is nothing wrong with spending money. It is a natural thing to spend and consume in the face of things you want. It is unnatural to control the flow of money and say no to some things. Discipline is required. Once the discipline is learned, it becomes your new, normal behavior, and thus, a habit.

Good habits can be as powerful and effective in your life as bad ones. Think about this. Good money habits produce wealth and a life enriched by wealth. Bad habits produce the opposite. Which habits would you prefer to have? The habits you develop in your life are dependent on the underlying structures you have consciously or unconsciously put in place in your life.

Next, I wish to write about three more rules for controlling money and using it to create wealth. ■

The Science of Creating Wealth™

When I do seminars on **The Science of Creating Wealth**™, I am invariably asked for investment advice. *"How can I get a 9-12% return on my investments?"* is sure to come up, early and often. Would you like to hear how I answer that question?

The first thing I have to say, is a reminder. Unless you become a saver, you will never become an investor. A 20% return on nothing is nothing. If you saved nothing, you have nothing to invest.

The rules of creating wealth are easy enough to remember. Do you remember **Rule Two** from the last chapter? Rule Two says **"Save at least 10% of your income".** Saving 10% of your income is what makes it possible for you to become an investor.

Someone once said that for an investor the overriding concern is not WHAT return you get on your money but THAT you get your money returned. Now that you've put the structure and systems in place to save money to invest, it is very important that you don't use that money unwisely and lose it. You cannot create wealth with money you've lost. Let's make this the subject of another rule:

- **Rule #4. Never Lose Money.**

Each and every dollar spent must be thought of with some return in mind. To spend money with no thought of consequences nor demand of return is to act as a fool; to cause destruction and ruin. I'm not going to repeat the old saying about a fool and his money being quickly parted. You already know to be careful with your investment dollars, but I think some of you may still underestimate the risks. Don't ever think an investment can't be dangerous because a lot of other people have put money in it.

I remember I once had a broker tell me it was time to *"jump in and get my feet wet"* with some of the "hot" tech and internet stocks. This was, of course, just about a month before the bubble burst on those high-flyers and their stock prices tumbled down to a quarter or less of their price per share. Many people took huge losses in their portfolios.

The world of money and investments has more traps and pitfalls than any other place I know. "Jumping in" is always risky. Taking someone else's advice about what you should do when you aren't familiar with an investment is always a mistake. In the world of money and investments, you need to know what you are doing and be in control of yourself at all times. No exceptions.

A friend of mine took up mountain climbing in his 40's, a little old for that sport, but Bob was already a marathoner and a champion skier. I met him last July as he was preparing for a trip to Alaska. He and a partner were going to attempt some remote peak that had never been climbed. The route they had planned would be technically very challenging. I looked at his photos of the forbidding snow and ice-covered mountain. I listened to his frank description of the challenges and risks. I finally asked him one question. WHY? Why do such a dangerous thing? *"The thing I like best about being on a mountain,"* Bob replied, *"is the sense of control it gives me. Everything I do, everything, I think about first, and then I do it carefully and precisely. I am in complete control of everything I do on the mountain. The consequences of one careless act can be permanent."*

What does mountain climbing have to do with investing? I'm not suggesting that mountain climbing and investing are activities of comparable risk. I am suggesting that you need to think about where you put your foot and where you put your money. The risks may not be comparable, but the discipline should be the same. Know what you are doing and be in control of yourself at all times. People who invest emotionally and people who climb emotionally are prone to very costly mistakes.

I understand that it is hard to be Spock-like with your money. I want to write a little bit about the emotions investors are naturally prey to and how to deal with them. Protecting your money is mostly about being in control of your emotions.

I'm going to quote you a long passage because the words are so powerful and true. Read through it thoughtfully, perhaps several times. It is from Napoleon Hill's classic, **Think and Grow Rich.** Personally, I'd like to see the book entitled

Think Differently and Create Wealth. This section of the book is captioned **"The Most Destructive Fear".** Hill writes:

"Fear of poverty is a state of mind, nothing else! But it is sufficient to destroy one's chances of achievement in any undertaking. This fear paralyzes the faculty of reason, destroys the faculty of imagination, kills off self-reliance, undermines enthusiasm, discourages initiative, leads to uncertainty of purpose, encourages procrastination, wipes out enthusiasm and makes self-control an impossibility. It takes the charm from one's personality, destroys the possibility of accurate thinking, diverts concentration of effort; it masters persistence, turns the will-power into nothingness, destroys ambition, beclouds the memory and invites failure in every conceivable form; it kills love and assassinates the finer emotions of the heart, discourages friendship and invites disaster in a hundred forms, leads to sleeplessness, misery and unhappiness – and all this despite the obvious truth that we live in a world of over-abundance of everything the heart could desire, with nothing standing between us and our desires, except the lack of a definite purpose.

"The fear of poverty is without doubt the most destructive of the six basic fears. You would

think that a fear of poverty would make men (and women) tight and miserly with their money. It does for a few, but for most of them its effect is the opposite. It makes them reckless with their money. They "jump in" for fear of missing the investment of a lifetime. And they 'stampede out' on rumors that there is a problem.

"Fear of poverty is at the top of the list of destructive fears because it is the most difficult to master. The fear of poverty grew out of man's instinctive tendency to prey upon his fellow man. Nearly all lower animals are motivated by instinct, but their capacity to think is limited. As a result, they tend to prey upon one another physically. Man, with his superior capacity to think and reason, conceives of his fellow man as prey in a broader sense. The form of predation that satisfies him is economic, not physical. Man, in fact, is so naturally predatory that just about every conceivable law has been passed to try to protect human prey from human predator. You tell me whether you think our system of laws has checked predation and exploitation".

You need to keep these unpleasant facts about human psychology in mind when you venture into the arena of investments. Think of it as an arena. If you think you're going to make a "killing" overnight in some investment, wise up. You are probably walking into a trap set by someone more clever and predatory than you. If you need to feel like you are beating the house and outsmarting everyone else, you are gambling, not investing. You are using your money emotionally for other purposes than creating wealth. Which leads to rule 5.

- **Rule #5. Never Gamble or Become Emotional With Your Money.**

Not all psychologists agree that gambling or speculating is fear-based behavior. I think no emotion but fear is strong enough to drive people into reckless behavior with their money. People who gamble, or jump into risky ventures, are sometimes very intelligent people. They KNOW the odds are bad, yet they play.

Do risky investments scare you but also attract you? Do you like the feeling of being "in the action" and being a "player" in the investment game. All of this, I will say again, is strongly incompatible with creating wealth. People who invest emotionally and in high risk instruments do not create wealth. They end up where all gamblers end up.

Please don't shrug all this off with the thought that you aren't a gambler. I understand that you don't think of yourself as a gambler. But you don't need to go to Vegas or bet the sports line to be a gambler. If you put money emotionally into risky instruments, you are gambling, not investing. You are putting your money in danger, not protecting it.

Over the years, I've talked to thousands of professionals.

The Science of Creating Wealth™

I regret to tell you that I've met only a few who were truly serious, disciplined, and diligent with regard to their investments. Far too many effectively gamble with their money, committing it emotionally and without a reasonable aversion to risk. Many also give their money to money managers who gamble with their money as well. The problem is that people think these managers can beat the market. Less than 5% do in any 10 year period of time.

Markets are often not always efficient. Buyers do not know the games sellers are playing. There is more deception in the arena of investments than in any other area I know. I am writing this book for professionals who make their income over an extended period of time, 20 to 35 years, or even 40 years. The good news for people with this sort of planned growth is that they can afford to let their money grow slowly and safely over a longer period of time. There is no need to be gambling! If you structure your life and practice so that you save 5% or more of your gross income, the return of your money is more important than the return on your money.

Some years ago, just when the technology and internet bubble was starting to burst, a doctor said to me *"I don't want to be in this market. I know this is going to get ugly, but inflation is going to eat me alive if I get out and try to stay conservative. I have to stay in the market."* Fear of poverty was driving this man to play in an arena he didn't want to be in and didn't need to be in. Inflation was a worry, not a reality in 2000-2005. Inflation has been mostly under control in the

U.S. economy for more than 25 years. Rises in the cost of goods and labor have been modest and matched by rises in income. This is very good news for investors and for business owners. This means that controlling expenses in business or a practice is not a losing game for professionals. Goods and wages are not spiraling upward at a rate that undercuts planning and savings.

I think it was Warren Buffet who said if you wish to become an astute investor in a business, it's an excellent idea first to become an astute owner of a business. Running your own business is an excellent reality check. A successful business owner has already learned the worries and concerns of owning a business. We are blessed with an economy that has both stable growth and low inflation. That is the optimal environment for a professional who wants to grow his business and save without taking high risks. People sometimes have the misfortune to live in stagnant economies with high inflation. They are forced to become gamblers to grow their business and create wealth. We aren't.

I agree with Buffet on the basis of my own years of experience with professionals and their businesses. My partner in our Life Planning program also seconds these observations. He says this correlation is not at all surprising. Astute investors were first successful business owners because successful owners know they must always be in control of their money and make their decisions in a rational, business-like, (not emotional) way.

The Science of Creating Wealth™

What rule are we discussing here? Isn't it **Rule #4: Never Lose Money?** I have been focusing on risky investments, but isn't there another area in which you, as a professional, must be no less careful and in control? Isn't the money you produce in your business or practice *your* money? So guard it from loss due to out of control expenses and overpaid taxes. Structure the costs of your business and taxes so that the flow of money favors you!

As a professional, your business or practice is the source of the money you have to invest. If your business has good revenue, but by the time the money flows to your bottom line and you have nothing left to invest, you aren't protecting your money. The underlying structure of money, which controls the flow of money, is faulty. Every professional should be generating enough income to make investments. If you don't know why your money is vanishing before the bottom line, you may wish to call in a business or practice consultant. In 30 years, I've never seen a practice that couldn't be improved, provided the structures were changed. Expenses are out of control, taxes are being overpaid, too much or the wrong kind of debt is being supported – some or all of these problems are consuming your potential to save and invest. Take action on this today. Protect the money your hard work is earning. And, last, but not least, Rule 6.

- **Rule #6. Invest In What You Need**
  Rather Than What You Want."
  Put your money toward what you NEED in life, things

such as home prepayment, food, clothing, transportation, retirement, and an emergency fund. More excellent advice. It is very common for those who have not made a fundamental choice to create wealth to increase their personal spending for what they WANT instead of what they NEED. People who overspend and over consume often say things like *"We really don't spend that much money. We are really conservative in what we buy."* So where does all the money go? I won't call these people delusional, but I will say they just aren't aware of the poor money habits controlling their life.

It doesn't matter how much you make, how carefully you manage your business, if your personal spending is out of control and consumes everything you make and maybe more than you make. There will be nothing left to save or invest! ■

CHAPTER 12 ■

Safe Investing

"Those who aim to create wealth
must first learn not to lose money."

I've often been asked to write about my experiences with money and creating wealth. I wanted to write about creating wealth but didn't want to write a "how-to" book. There are too many of those out there already. And I didn't want to write a book that seemed to be preaching. I'm not some all-knowing financial guru, but a person just like you who has had to study, learn and practice the discipline of creating wealth. I've been successful at it because I've recognized the masters of wealth creation and studied the actions and habits of master wealth creators. This does not mean that I know it all or that I'm better than anyone else. It simply means I have developed the knowledge, skills and discipline and put the structure in my life and business to create wealth. I can tell you how to obtain the same skills, but I can't create wealth for you. Only YOU can do that. Only you can have the desire and inner drive to create wealth and abundance in your life. You are in charge of your life, not me.

It's a cliché, but I'm going to use it: *"creating wealth*

isn't brain surgery or rocket science". What I want you to understand and believe is how really simple it is to create wealth. You may have doubts about that right now, but once you start creating wealth you'll understand. I'm going to give you some simple examples of how to do this.

Many of you have lost money in complicated investment schemes. Many of you have never really been serious about saving and investing. Many of you have spent the money you should have invested. Isn't this the truth? Keeping it simple is a better way to conduct every aspect of your life. Generally, the more money you make, the more complicated your life and business tends to become. But you don't have to let this happen.

Keeping things simple has many rewards. You will discover that you will have more money if you choose to live a simpler life. You will discover you have more time to focus on the important things. Learning to live on less than you make is a critical first step toward create wealth.

I'm going to tell you about Tom, a professional who continues to violate most of the principles of creating wealth. Tom's story is a lesson for all of us.

Tom is a specialist, a surgeon in private practice, with a gross income of $1.4 million dollars. Tom is 54 years old and married. He lives in a $900,000 home with a $350,000 mortgage. In his four car garage you will find not one, but two, expensive German sports cars. He and his wife spend about $450,000 a year on their lifestyle. They like to travel to exotic places three or four times a year.

In 24 years, Tom has only managed to save or invest $750,000 for his retirement. He has a condition that could put an end to his ability to practice dentistry in 7 years or less. The medications he takes to slow his disability are taking a toll on his health. When I asked Tom if he was willing to curtail his lifestyle in anticipation of becoming disabled, his answer was a resounding, *"No way!"*.

I reminded Tom of our **"Rule of 20"** for funding retirement: One needs to put away at least 20 to 25 times what you are currently spending in order to retire at that same level of income. For Tom, (who manages to spend about a half million dollars a year), twenty times his current spending averages around ten million dollars, or more precisely, $9,000,000 to $11,250,000! Think about that. To continue to support the kind of lifestyle he has manufactured for himself, in retirement Tom would need to set aside about nine or ten million dollars.

How do you think he's doing? So far Tom has saved $750,000. If it's a good year this year (and the Porsche dealer doesn't talk him into a new car), he hopes to contribute another $100,000 to savings. I think, barring a lottery win, there is no way Tom will ever make it to nine or ten million. Not in this lifetime or the next. Why? Because Tom consumes almost all the money his fine practice generates. His savings and investing rate is so low he would need 70 rather than 7 years to fund his retirement.

Tom is an excellent surgeon. The focus of his practice is

quality-based care. He operates his business with honesty and integrity, but he is just not creating financial freedom and wealth for himself. The reason he isn't, and can't, is that Tom has not learned to apply even one principle of creating true wealth in his life. His lifestyle of high consumption and high taxes is completely undermining any financial strategy that could create wealth. Even now, Tom could have elected to put away $150,000 a year in a defined benefit plan, plus another $40,000 in 401K plans, but instead he prefers to continue to consume rather than create wealth.

You are probably thinking, *"Wow, why am I reading about this willful, financially irresponsible guy? This isn't my story. I don't consume and consume and refuse to save. I want to create wealth in my life!"*

No, this isn't your story, but can you identify with the financial habits that are undermining Tom's future? It's a matter of degree of course, but we all tend to over consume and under save with the pressures of maintaining a lifestyle. It is a sad statistic, but true: **More than 90% of professional men and women who own their own businesses don't have enough control of their money to create wealth.**

I wanted to write this book because we all have a story to tell. Some of us have done a better job than Tom in preparing for our futures. Some of us have done about the same or worse. We all are writing our own story. My purpose for this book was to create a dialog that would allow anyone who reads it the ability for self-study and self-evaluation. You

The Science of Creating Wealth™

can't read about someone like Tom without thinking about your own situation.

Modern psychology wonders and worries about our capacity for free choice. Are we "free" to overcome attitudes, old habits and structures that have become ingrained over many years? I know we can overcome our bad habits. Yes, we are born already pre-disposed to make choices in certain ways. Yes, most of us have been deeply influenced by our parents and our schooling, by what life and living have shown us, and by what our role models and mentors taught us. From this combination of innate disposition and life conditioning, we developed a unique set of habits, preferences, beliefs, desires, values, and dreams. These determine our day-to-day life choices. None of this is set in concrete. We can change our preferences, desires and beliefs. We can clarify our values. We can replace structures in our life that are failing with structures that can ensure success. People do make these changes throughout their lives.

Our financial habits and choices are no exception. Certainly they are heavily influenced by the same factors. But, we can change our attitude toward money. Whatever financial choices we made yesterday, we can make different ones today. If we want a better future, we know we need to make better decisions today. This is something we can do, but it requires new knowledge, new training and new thinking, a full-court commitment to a different way of dealing with money. What I'm trying to do here is show you the changes you can make.

Owning your own business immediately adds complexity to your life. When you work for someone else, your employer determines when you work, what you do, and what you make. If you work in a good place, then you also get some company-paid benefits. All of these things you have to provide for yourself when you're self-employed. You have to set up some sort of 401K or pension plan into which you make automatic and mandatory contributions. You have to establish a mechanism and a discipline of savings. The government, or your employer does not do it for you. Not that people who work for others don't get into trouble by failing to save – they do – but the complexity of the financial structure they are dealing with is a great deal simpler.

Every professional normally generates enough income to make investments. Once you've designed the structures that will put you in control of your money and increase your net profits, you have a choice. This is where the rubber meets the road. By using sound principles to control your money, you will change your life forever. You can instantly break away from the pack – the 90% who are over consuming and being taxed into oblivion. You can stop being someone who is stuck working harder and harder, producing more and more, but never managing to create a secure future. You can move into the top 10% and break away from the production mentality. Once you are in the top 10%, you can then move into the top 3%!

When you make more money, you can do one of two things. You can spend and consume more, or you can save and invest more. One path leads to creating wealth, the other path leads to the stress, distress, overwork, and the other "unpleasant" consequences of having failed to create financial independence. It's your choice. Each day and every day you make choices. The choices you and your spouse and family make now will determine your future.

When my clients start investing, I always urge them to take a consistent and conservative approach. Insiders can sometimes beat the market averages (indexes), but less than 5% of all money managers do so over any 10 year period. A return of 9-12% per year is a very reasonable target for a conservative investor. A conservative investor, remember, is one whose first priority is to conserve his capital.

I suggest you use 9% per year as your rule of thumb for projecting growth. To get a rough estimate of how long it will take your money to double at a given annual rate, divide the rate into 72. So, if your annual rate of return is 9%, since 72 divided by 9 equals 8, it will take you about eight years to double your money. This assumes, I should add, that your money is growing in a tax deferred environment and not being reduced annually by a healthy tax bite.

If you invest every month in a consistent and conservative fashion, you don't run the risk of significant losses. Younger people, it is said, should be willing to accept greater risk, but I've never understood this idea promoted by financial planners. If you have the time to build wealth conservatively, why risk losses at any age. Risk, remember, measures the probability that you won't achieve your objective.

If your goal is wealth, you don't want to lose 25% of your invested capital. This means it would take you 3-5 years of normal growth to simply restore the principle you've lost. Looking back at my investment career, which now is over 40 years, I see how the consistent compounding of low risk returns far outweighs the uncertain, volatile returns of high risk investments. I could write several books just about the horror stories I've heard. Good people are given bad advice, or no advice, and act on their own with little or no knowledge of what they were investing in. Predictable results follow. Many suffer serious losses and give up on saving and investing altogether.

Read this line several times: *"Some day, I too, am going to be 55 or 60, or 65!"* Will I be in a position of financial freedom, or will I still be tied to the chair, the desk, or my business? Will I be financially free or "chained to the chair"? Remember, just because you have created wealth doesn't mean you won't want to work and won't enjoy working. It simply means you won't have to work.

A local orthodontist to whom I have referred clients, told me his story. He said he lost over 50% of the money he had invested with a broker, and then quit saving and investing altogether. He said, *"I invest in my own body and don't trust anyone else."* Guess what? He's in his sixties now and still working long hours. He'll be working until he drops, and not because he wants to, but because he has to. This is the legacy of failing to save and invest to create wealth.

I'd rather you err on the side of being a little too conservative. But there is a price to pay for being ultra-conservative. If your savings grow at the rate of 5-6% per year, it means you'll need 13 years to double your principle. 26 years to double again, rather than 16 years.

A long term strategy that targets 9-12% per year with low risk is the best strategy for professionals and small business owners with a good income stream. You can reasonably expect to create wealth within a 12-20 year horizon. The pace at which you create wealth will depend on how much you consume. The higher your lifestyle, the more money you'll have to put away. The more you consume, the slower your pace in creating wealth.

So, how do you find a 9-12% per year strategy? The first thing you must keep in mind is safety. You must invest only where your principle is relatively safe, only were it may be reclaimed when you want, and only where you'll get a fair return. Safety and liquidity are of course matters of degree.

I often recommend that busy professionals work with advisors, but only with advisors who have already amassed considerable wealth themselves. Otherwise, you have people using your money to learn. Working with rookies in the financial arena is a recipe for failure, if not disaster. Seasoned veterans know the ropes and can offer you advice based on "having been there" themselves. Beginners haven't been investing money long enough to fully understand the risks in what they may be recommending. They haven't seen what

Mandelbrot likes to call the inevitable fluctuations of the markets over longer periods of time. Rookies think the future will always be like the present. It won't be. Things can and will change in an instant, as they did September 11, 2001.

Many financial advisors with short track records are also more interested in making money from you than for you. Of all the investment newsletters that are sold and promoted, not one has beaten the S&P Index over any 15 year period of time. The quick in-and-out traders always lose to the long-term investors.

Many brokers and investment advisors, you need to keep in mind, haven't learned how to create wealth for themselves, or for you. They are in-and-out traders, far more interested in the commissions they can make from overtrading your portfolio than in the money they make for you. In the jargon of Wall Street, they *"churn and burn."* By the way, you are the one who gets burned!

I've always believed that investment advisors should get a bigger percentage of the profits they create. But, by the same logic, they should also take a share of the losses. I find it interesting that not one investment house or advisor I've ever met is willing to share in the losses that come from following their advice. Curious, isn't it, that they are unwilling to risk even part of their compensation on performance!

The investment advisor community is far too biased in favor of the advisor making money regardless of results. Advisors know, that over time, their clients must make money. Otherwise, they'll move their money, right? But, many people are slow and reluctant in leaving "trusted" advisors even if that person or firm isn't making them money. I've spoken with professionals, time and time again, who were paying for advice from large financial institutions but had lost year after year based on following that advice. One doctor I counseled, had lost over $350,000 of his original $900,000 investment before he moved his money. I don't think he would have even then, if I hadn't taken the time to sit down with him and review the abysmal record of the previous 4 years. It's amazing to see how often working professionals are abused by the investment community.

Protect your money. Put it in the hands of people who understand how to create wealth. Find out whether your broker or advisor invests in the same instruments that he recommends to you. If he doesn't, why doesn't he? Get references from other clients who have worked with him. If he can't give you references, move on. You are better off putting your money in CD's than in the hands of a bad advisor. At least with CD's your only risk is inflation.

There isn't a good financial advisor today who doesn't use the major indexes as a benchmark for investing your money. Not one. If you can do as well as the major indexes after fees, you are doing very well. Some people become emotionally attached to their investments. This is one of the main reasons I recommend index investing. People don't tend to become attached to their index fund or index shares in the way they get attached to a particular stock. I remember someone in 2000 saying *"I love my Cisco and I'll never sell it."* That emotional reaction cost them a lot of money!

Love your spouse. Love your family. Love what you do, but don't fall in love with your investments. If you can take emotions out of investing, you have a much better chance of winning. For this reason alone, I am for using financial advisors, but if you do, you'd better keep track of what they are doing and meet with them every 3 months. That's right, if you aren't looking at your investments every three months, then no one can help you, not me or anyone else.

I'm not here to pressure you into any particular kind of investment, or to tell you what you must do, or who to use, or to avoid advisors. That depends on you and on the time and market savvy you have. Some of you may know more about the financial markets than I do. What I do say is this, any advisor you use had better be able to beat the indexes by at least 3-4%, because that is what managing your money will cost you. If your advisor can't outperform the market by enough to cover his management fees, aren't you better off investing in (no load) index fund or shares?

As I said, index funds are not for everyone, and there are financial advisors that can and do beat these averages over time. These advisors are well worth the fees they charge, but in my personal opinion and research, they are few and far between. I know of several, but unless you can find the best, you are probably better off keeping things simple and using index funds. ∎

CHAPTER 13 ■
Smart People Die Rich

"Compound interest is the 8th
wonder of the world." — *Einstein*

You have created wealth when you have enough income to support your lifestyle whether you work or not. This is the best applied definition of wealth I know. One of the essential skills in building wealth is learning how to make compounding work for you. Professionals and small business owners need to invest part of their profits and let the returns from these investments compound over a period of years. Professionals and small business owners generally don't have enough income to create wealth without investing.

Let me tell you a story about trying to create wealth without investing. Recently, I was on a two week motorcycle trip with good friends in the Northwest. We had breakfast one morning at an Original Pancake House. The owner came by the table to visit with us. It was interesting conversation. She told us that she was selling her beautiful new house on 10 acres so she could build another Pancake House. Stop and think about this for a minute. She and her husband had built their dream home only a few years ago, and now she was selling it. Can you guess why? She was selling her dream home because she didn't have enough income to support it and the rest of her expensive lifestyle. She was selling her home because she decided she needed the money to create another *income-producing* asset.

Her idea of creating another income-producing asset, another Pancake House, was a good one, but think about her situation. What was happening to all her income from the current restaurant? Wasn't it being consumed in feeding her expensive lifestyle? She wasn't able to save anything because she was spending all the profits. In fact, because the profits from the one restaurant weren't enough, she was going to go out and create another profit-generating business. Where do you think the profits from the second restaurant are going to go?

Do you see what's wrong? The owner is a person who knows how to develop a business and generate income. That she does well, but that is only one piece of the puzzle in place. To create wealth you first must make money; but then, you must keep some of that money and put it where it will grow. The restaurant owner doesn't keep her money. Instead of saving and investing, she just consumes her income.

What she's doing means she will remain part of the 90% that will never create wealth. No matter how long she works, no matter how many restaurants she builds, she will never create wealth until she controls her spending and starts to save.

The owner said to me at one point, *"I work very hard*

but I never seem to have enough money". That is when I understood why she had this money problem. She was one of those people who always thinks about money as something of which she will never have enough. No matter how much some people make or have, they never have enough. Money is not their friend.

Does it seem odd to you to think about money in these terms? Think about the idea of money as your friend for a moment. Suppose you felt money was your friend. If you'd have a positive relationship with money, it would ramify throughout your life. You'd be making plans. You'd be thinking positively about your future. You'd be hopeful. You'd even have faith that there would be plenty to go around and you'd get your fair share.

If money is your friend, then it is not a foe to be conquered and seized. If money is your friend, it is something to be used and enjoyed; but also, an item of which you take care. We take care of our friends, don't we?

What I'm asking you to consider is whether our relationship with money should be positive rather than adversarial. Positive means we should be grateful for what we have and also a good steward of it. In order to have a good relationship with anything, we need to take care of it, maintain it, and protect it. Maybe you've never thought of money in this way, but maybe you should.

Money is a material asset that has enormous emotional and even spiritual overtones to it. Some people spend money to feel good; just like others drink alcohol and take drugs. In fact, as the author of **Money as a Drug** argues, money is an addiction for some people. The money addict can never get enough of the green stuff. He needs higher and higher doses to feel good.

An addiction to money is something to avoid, but we can't avoid money. Money is an important part of everyone's life. It influences, in one way or another, much of what we do. Since we have to deal with money, we cannot avoid an ongoing relationship with it. The trick is to cultivate the right relationship, because a bad relationship will cause problems in almost every area of your life.

Some people worry about money all the time. Everything in their life seems focused on money, and there's never enough. It's as if money worries were in control, and they were living their lives in permanent scarcity-survival mode.

Several years ago, a long-time client of The Schuster Center came back to lecture to his peers. He was an orthodontist. He started off his speech by saying, *"95% of orthodontists are in survival mode because of money. No matter now much they make, it's never enough."*

I hope he's wrong about the percentage, but he's not wrong about the many professionals having serious money problems. Why do some professionals fear that they will never earn enough or have enough?

Part of the answer, is that they won't subject themselves to the discipline of sitting down and figuring out what it

The Science of Creating Wealth™

actually costs them to live their current lifestyle. $10,000 per month? $20,000 per month? $25,000? Until you do this and get a handle on what really is going out the door, you have no idea how much you need to take in. You don't know how much you need to earn, and because you don't know, no level of income seems safe to you. Fear keeps telling you: Maybe you need a little more and a little more and a little more.

Despite the fact that you take in $20M to $50M over the lifetime of your business or practice, it may not seem enough to you. If you own a small business, you could be taking in $2.5 million year. Yet, because of how you think, it still does not seem enough to you.

We'll come back to this exercise of sitting down and figuring out what you really need. I think I've probably said enough about bad relationships with money. The pathology is fascinating, but what we need to do is talk about building a good relationship with money. I strongly suggest that you think about money as a friend. Think about money as something that will return the favor and help you, if you handle it in the right way. Money can help you because it grows if you put it in a safe place. It grows by compounding. That is what I want to explain to you now, how money grows by compounding.

When Einstein said that compound interest is *"the 8th wonder of the world"*, he surely meant it as a joke. But, joke or not, it works because compound interest is a very fundamental principle in using money, whether you borrow it and the compounding works AGAINST you, or whether you save and invest it and the compounding works FOR you.

Let me review with a few examples of how money rewards you if you save it and invest it in a safe place. Let's say you are a small business owner and things are starting to go well. You find you can put away $5,000 a month. You start building a portfolio of index funds and you keep this up for 5 years. You earn about 9% a year on your portfolio. Some easy arithmetic tells us that by the sixth year you are already receiving $34,645 per year in passive income. That's nearly $3,000 a month – twice your potential Social Security check.

You keep going with your $5,000 per month investing for another 5 years. After the 10th year of investing $5,000 a month at 9%, you have accumulated almost a million dollars ($979,828) and have a potential passive income of $88,184 per year. That's $7,333 per month without touching the principal!

You have created wealth using the principle of compound interest. Year after year, your gains keep compounding. That's the "secret". If you make 9% one year but then lose 15% the next, you can never get compounding working for you. Put your money in a safe place and let it grow year after year.

If you've been applying the principles in this book, you've learned to do three things:

(1) First, you learned to earn money by creating significant value for the people you serve.

(2) Second, you learned how to keep more of what you earn.

The Science of Creating Wealth™

(3) Third, you learned you must save and invest your money conservatively.

When you conserve your money, you can take advantage of compound interest. The returns we just looked at could be your numbers. For many of you, the numbers could even be better.

Let me give you another example. Suppose you could invest $10,000 a month at 9% interest. In 10 years you'd have compounded your way to $1,959,656, almost $2M dollars. You'd have a passive income of $176,369 per year or $14,700 per month without touching your $2M nest egg. You'd have created wealth in 10 years.

I know that many of you can't save $10,000 a month at this time. You don't need to save at that rate. You have time to create wealth at a slower rate. Compounding is the principle that works at whatever rate of saving and investing you can manage.

I hope none of you are still asking the question, *"Where am I going to find the money to invest?"* I wrote about three areas earlier when I was explaining budgets. I'm going to remind you of those areas.

Let's look again at an $800,000 a year professional practice. In today's dollars, that's no big deal. I said that 10% could be reclaimed in any practice using my Wealth Creation strategies. 10% of $800,000 is $80,000 per year, or nearly $6,700 per month. That's a slam dunk. At The Schuster Center, we have taught that to our clients for years and never has one come back and said *"I can't do it"*.

I also said that 20% of your tax bill could be saved with a coordinated financial strategy. A coordinated financial strategy takes into consideration your business and personal budgets as well as your tax and pension planning. It looks at how you can optimize your tax-deductible savings with a properly designed pension account. The money that could be saved with a good tax plan at the $800,000 income level amounts on average to nearly $30,000 per year.

$80,000 in business overhead savings plus $30,000 in tax savings adds up to $110,000 a year. But there's still one more source of savings. Remember the home budget we recommended? Implement that and you can keep your lifestyle but save an additional $10,000 a year. Add that $10,000 to the $110,000, and you get a total savings of $120,000 per year or $10,000 a month. That was the dollar amount we used in the example we looked at earlier. By investing $10,000 per month, you will reach $2M in ten years. At that point, you can take $14,700 in passive income per month without touching the $2M. You have created wealth in 10 years.

I'm not overlooking taxes in these calculations. The entire $120,000 per year can be sheltered in well designed pension and retirement plans. This takes some skill in pension plan design, but it is something you can do with good advice. The key is a sound comprehensive wealth plan, not a piecemeal approach to investing, savings, taxes, and retirement planning.

Have I answered your question about where to find the money you need to invest and create wealth? I understand that everyone's needs and circumstances are different. Off-the-shelf plans don't suit most people. At The Schuster Center, we don't try to shoehorn you into an off-the-shelf plan. Call The Schuster Center and ask for a coaching call with me (1-800-288-9393). Tell us about your situation, and we'll be happy to arrange a call that will give you some personalized direction and guidance.

As you proceed, I'd like you to keep something in mind. Unless you first make a fundamental commitment to create wealth in your life, none of this will happen. You won't take the necessary actions. You will continue to go down the path already in place. You will hesitate and procrastinate, and money will continue to run through your hands like water.

It is in your hands. I remember something Dick Fabian told me years ago. *"If you have a problem and the problem can be solved by money (and you have money or access to it), you have no problem!"* Let money solve the problems it can solve. Buy the expert help you need. I do!

I'd also like you to think about this: There are many competent and ethical accountants, financial planners, attorneys and money managers. However, not everyone who works in these professions is competent or ethical; but the bad apples can be spotted. Because of your position, because of your income and your income potential, you can find whatever help you need. Just take the time to do your own due diligence.

I remember a patient of mine named Ralph. Ralph got me interested in flying in 1981. We flew together on several occasions. He became a good friend like many of my patients.

Ralph had a very interesting problem. He had created awesome wealth. He owned 10,000 acres at Wolf Creek Pass in Colorado and a 2,400 acre ranch at the base of the pass. I stayed at his ranch several times. It was an incredible place. As Ralph was getting on in years, one day he confided in me that he was really in a bind. He wanted to will the property to his children, but if he did, the inheritance taxes would be so high that they would bankrupt all four of them. Fortunately, I knew a man who had dealt with a similar problem. I called him and he gave me the name of his attorney. I put Ralph in touch with the attorney. Several trusts were created in advance of Ralph's death and the entire property ultimately passed to his children tax free.

"If you have a problem and the problem can be solved by getting good professional help, then you have no problem." This has been proven true in my life on many occasions, and I've seen it work in many other lives.

Wealth is something you can create in your life, but you need some understanding of how to do it. The "What I Want" always comes before the "Why I Want It" and the "How Do I Get It". This is how our mind works. When our intellect, (knowing what we want), is synergistically empowered by our emotions, (driving why we want it), our behavior is relatively reliable and predictable. Human behavior has changed very little in the past 600 years! Through research, study, and application, we know more today about human behavior than ever before.

We are fortunate that our system of government

provides the opportunity for intelligent people to create wealth.

We can avail ourselves of the assistance of tax advisors, accountants, financial planners and money managers. There are always ways for professionals and business owners to lower their taxes. The key is to build an entire system in which all of the parts are working synergistically to help you create wealth and freedom. We can use our businesses as wealth-creating machines. We should use them in that way rather than as lifestyle-creating machines. Financial freedom is something any of us can achieve in 120 months or less. Letting your investment dollars compound tax-free in sheltered accounts is the key.

"Smart People don't die broke, they die rich!" ∎

The Science of Creating Wealth™

"If it's your money or your life, choose life."

"We (the lenders) own it all. All of it. The businesses out there. You the borrowers just run these businesses for us. You guys run them for us, the financial institutions."

— (quoted from **The Millionaire Mind)**

I began speaking and writing about creating wealth in 1974. I was very excited about what I was discovering and applying in my own life. I knew the principles of creating wealth would have a huge impact on the life of anyone who accepted and practiced them. For the most part, people were very receptive to my ideas, but in one area I met with a surprising deal of resistance. That's the subject I am about to discuss.

I don't know what you're thinking right now. I don't know whether you've powered through this book or whether you're on some kind of chapter-a-month program. That's up to you. I believe you'd get the most out of this book if you powered through it once, and then go back and study it maybe chapter-by-chapter or principle-by-principle. If you've done it that way, I'd be willing to bet that your thinking has already changed quite a bit by now.

When I start talking about debt and getting out of debt, I can feel the uneasiness and discomfort in my audience. My beliefs and strategies about debt and debt reduction go against traditional thinking. Or, at least against what most of us have been taught to believe.

I'm sure you understand that I'm not writing this book to upset people. I'm writing it because I know anyone can create wealth if they learn and apply these principles. That's my message to you and my purpose in writing this book. What I'm offering you is a science, not speculation and hype.

Let me begin with some statements and see whether we can find common ground, as if we were in the same room visiting with each other. I'd like you to think about what we are doing here as having a conversation.

First, I am assuming that you, like me, are working somewhere in the professional world. We both know about what's involved in running our own business. Professionals and business owners are the target audience for which this books is addressed. Not that these principles won't work for people who are employed. They work for everyone, but in some situations they take longer to work. I am hoping many more aspiring entrepreneurs who are striving to own their own business will find great benefits in this book BEFORE they make costly errors in judgment.

Second, your work life is finite. You have only so many

years to work and produce and accumulate what you can. Actuaries have the delightful little term "YPLs", (years of productive life). Professionals tend to average about 35-40 YPLs. Long enough, but not enough to waste 20 or 25 years in unproductive activities.

Third, people who take care of themselves – those who don't smoke or drink, and who eat right, exercise and reduce stress – can work longer and live longer. You know you have important choices to make. You have to decide what you will do about eating, exercising, and dealing with stress. These choices will have real consequences for how long you can live and work.

Fourth, the amount of money that you will make in your lifetime is determined by your profession, your business abilities, and your goals. Dentists in the U.S., for example have average annual earnings of about $135,000. More than 90% of dentists make within $40,000 of this mean, but some make a great deal more. Abilities and goals matter.

Fifth, the money you make comes for the most part in increments. The daily amount has an average. The monthly amount has an average. The quarterly and yearly amounts can be averaged. It is probably most useful to think about your income in terms of these averages.

Sixth, few of us take a long and careful look at where all our money is going. All we know is that it keeps going – business expenses, personal lifestyle expenses, interest on loans, and taxes. Because it keeps going out, it has to keep coming in. We can increase our income up to a certain point, but beyond that point we lose all quality of life trying to make more money. Also, for most of us, the complexity of running our business becomes overwhelming at a certain point.

Seventh, debt can be all consuming of income. Debt is something we must use, but also must control. To achieve wealth and the freedom it brings, you must have a plan to get out of debt on terms that favor you, not the bank or other lenders.

If more than 20% of your personal income is consumed by debt interest, regardless of what the debt is for, you are too far in debt and should implement a plan to lower your debt. If your interest payments in your business are greater than 10% of income, then your business has too much debt, no matter what type of debt.

Debt is something we can and must control as owners of our own businesses and Masters of our own destiny. Out of control debt will devour all of your profits. Think of a dollar of debt as a dollar of lost profit, or as a dollar that could have gone to savings and investments especially if that dollar were a tax deductible retirement contribution.

Debt is not necessarily bad. I am not preaching against all debt. I am, however, preaching for having a plan to eliminate debt on favorable terms. Borrowing money must be better for you than for the bank.

Think about debt as compound interest working against you; and, you will have an exact picture of what debt really is. Somewhere, somehow, it seems to have crept into the American psyche that being in debt is something good or least O.K. In the last few years, millions of people rushed out to buy an expensive home, as much house as the lenders would allow them, with little or no down payment. They were completely sold on the idea that home ownership is a wise investment and better in every way than renting. The huge mortgage debt they were assuming didn't matter. Debt is your friend!

Well, as long as the value of residential real estate was rising faster than the mortgage rate, it made sense to own an expensive home with borrowed money. But real estate prices are cyclical. After a run-up has gone on for a while, buyers exhaust their credit and can buy no more. Sellers find no buyers and cannot carry their heavily mortgaged property indefinitely. Prices have to fall to attract any buyers. The value of your home may decline significantly. You may quickly find yourself owing more than your home is worth.

Don't worry. Real estate investment is cyclical and prices will come back. Just sit tight. But suppose your income declines, or you have to move, or you have some other major expenses with which to deal? You are probably going to have to sell your expensive house and in the process be forced to take a serious loss to clear the debt. The "investment" you made in an expensive home with borrowed money (debt) proved to be a costly financial mistake. All of this was absolutely predictable.

Everyone should know how debts, like home and car

loans, are structured. When you get a loan, the loan is front-loaded with interest. Your early payments build little or no equity in what you've purchased.

Here's an example of what I mean. This is the negative effect of COMPOUND DEBT.

$200,000 Loan at 11%, Payments of $1,904/Month For 30 years

Yr	Interest Paid per yr	Principal Paid per yr	Mortgage Balance End of yr	Average Interest per mo	Average Principal per mo
1	$21,955	$900	$199,099	$1,830	$75
5	$21,460	$1,395	$194,329	$1,798	$116
10	$20,443	$2,412	$184,525	$1,703	$201
15	$18,685	$4,170	$167,574	$1,557	$348
20	$15,645	$7,209	$138,268	$1,203	$601
25	$10,390	$12,465	$87,600	$866	$1,039
30	$1,305	$21,550	$ 0	$109	$1,796

Let's look at these numbers together. I have used five-year averages so that we have one number which represents the average for that 5 year period of time. You see immediately how little equity this loan generates for the homeowner in the first 5 years. Only $900 per year. $4,500 in five years. That is 2.25% of the purchase price. Suppose the homeowner needs to move within 5 years and the price of his house has declined 7.5%. Then, our homeowner faces a loss at sale of $10,500 plus costs. And he has had to maintain the property for 5 years. Great investment? I doubt it!

The numbers are unfavorable for any debtor and always favor the lender unless you borrow with the clear goal of creating wealth. This home loan is a wealth-producing instrument only in the special circumstances that residential real estate, like your home, appreciates faster than what the loan costs you. How likely is that, if the loan cost you 11% or even 6% per year?

Look again, at the first year. You paid a total of 12 times $1,904 or $22,848 for the year, of which $21,955 went to interest and $900 to principal. That is $22,000 lost to servicing debt. You can deduct it, but keep in mind that you have to produce the money to pay for it.

Remember, we said that you will only make so much money in your lifetime. How much of this money is going to be consumed by debt? You have school loans, business equipment loans, house loans, car loans, credit card loans, and consumer goods loans. If you aren't a wise debt manager, you can end up owing so much in interest that you have no money left to save or invest.

One last point about the $200,000 home loan. It isn't until sometime in the 23-24th year that the amount of principal paid equals the amount of interest paid. That is not a wealth-creating instrument. As I said, I'm not against borrowing money, but the repayment must favor you, not the lender.

If you are going to purchase a home with mortgage financing, here are some guidelines that target wealth creation.

Get a 30-year mortgage, but pay it off in 10 years. That will reduce the interest you pay on a 30-year note by 75%! You're better off paying this money to yourself in the form of deductible pension contributions than paying the high interest to the bank and deducting it. You can also deduct the payments you make to your wealth-creating pension plan.

A good strategy for paying off a 30-year loan in 10 years is to pay 133% of the term payment every month. For example, the monthly payment on our $200,000, 30-year mortgage was $1,904. Multiply that by 133% and you get $2,538. The extra $634 can be applied to the principal each month, and the loan will be finished in approximately 10 years.

Retiring the mortgage in 10 years is a good, balanced strategy for home purchases. In your business, I recommend no more than 10% of gross dollars be used to pay off debt. I don't, in general, recommend aggressive pay downs or pre-payments of business loans. The reason for the 10% guideline – and it can vary with individuals – is that if you pay more than 10% down on business loans, you'll have your income to pay taxes on, but you won't have the money (or be squeezed) to pay your taxes, because you are paying too much in loan pre-payment.

You could pay off the home loan we've been talking about in 5 years and pocket 85% of the interest you would have paid over 30 years. That aggressive pay down schedule requires you to double your monthly payments. If you can easily afford $3,808 per month, that's fine. Just be sure your current expenses are under control and your income can support an aggressive loan pre-payment plan. Don't forget about your taxes.

Different people hold different opinions on debt. The vast majority of people are debtors themselves and have come to believe that debt is good. Some financial experts recommend or accept a substantial debt load on young professionals. In my view, these experts don't know the first thing about true wealth creation or they wouldn't praise debt.

Allow me to share a story about a person I know very well. Several years ago he paid $8,000 to a leading financial planning firm to create a financial plan for he and his spouse. This is basically an accounting firm turned into a financial planning firm. My friend had asked them to help him pay off a loan early. The loan was part of a settlement with a former business partner. The loan was for $1,500,000 over 10 years. He was paying his ex-partner $15,000 a month including interest. There was an early pay-off clause in the contract.

The firm took my friend's $8,000 and came back to him with the advice that he shouldn't pre-pay this loan. The IRS wouldn't like it if he did.

Emotionally, my friend really wanted to pay the debt off. November of 1999 came and my friend had a tax payment due in April, 2000 for $368,000. My friend asked his personal accountant what he could do to avoid this payment. The answer was "pay off the loan". That is exactly what he had wanted to do, but had held off doing so on the advice of the financial firm who liked debt and promoted the idea that their clients produce like crazy and carry high debt. My friend didn't know about their views when he signed up with them.

To make a long story short, my friend pre-paid his ex-partner $450,000 and reduced his April $368,000 tax payment to virtually nothing. In January of 2000, he pre-paid the rest of the note, saving another $275,000. In two years, he had completely paid off the note, saving $275,000 in interest and nearly $650,000 in taxes.

Yes, my friend saved that amount in interest and taxes, and also gained something even more importantly. Can you guess what it was? How about peace of mind? You know, all the rules and guidelines in the world aren't important unless they give you peace of mind and let you sleep at night.

I, myself, am debt-averse. I've seen what excessive debt does to lives and businesses. I've seen what compulsive spending does to anyone addicted to it. I've seen the emotional drain that comes from mishandling money. I don't want debt to control my life.

Every person is different. None of us should accept "cookie-cutter" solutions that aren't right for our heads, our hearts and our souls. Don't let anyone sell you on a financial arrangement that makes you uncomfortable.

There is another popular myth about debt. Many professionals believe that debt is good because they can write off the interest. No debt means you will be paying higher taxes.

Let me dispose of this myth. Yes, you can write off debt.

No, you don't have to pay higher taxes if you carry no debt. Higher taxes result only if you don't avail yourself of pension strategies that allow you to put investment dollars away tax-free. You can spend your money paying debt, or you can use that same money to fund wealth-creating pensions. The tax consequences are the same. The wealth consequences are as different as night and day.

Not all the money you save and invest should be put in a tax-deferred pension; but. with proper business planning, combined with your master wealth plan, you can reclaim money that would have been lost to debt payments. You earn no more money, but with a smarter use of your existing funds, you turn money that would have been lost to servicing debt into money that is working for your own future.

Let me ask you something. When you went into business it was to work for yourself, right? Not the bank? Nor the IRS? Or, your employees? Let me remind you of the metaphor with which I began this book. Your practice or your business is your oil well. Use what it produces well. What you do with the money that comes out of your business is in your hands. Use this money wisely and it will serve you well. Waste it and it will become your master.

"Master of money or slave to money is a life choice." ■

The Science of Creating Wealth™

CHAPTER 15 ■
Creating Wealth Is Simple
But Not Easy!

This little book has an astonishing message. Maybe you've got it by now, but I'd be willing to bet that many of you haven't. Let me call it **The Wealth Secret.**

Remember, first that there are two basic life orientations that you can choose. You can choose to be a *creative* or a *reactive* person. A creative person plans and creates the business and the life he wants for himself. He is in control. A reactive person is stuck trying to deal with the problems that surround him. He is not in control, his problems are.

The Wealth Secret is about how money flows into and out of your life. Either you control the flow of money in your life or your money controls you. It's that simple! A creative person is in control of his money and makes it work for him. A reactive person is forever struggling with money as a problem that is out of control.

My colleague, Stephen Covey, the modern day Dale Carnegie, says we must be *pro-active*. That is the first "Habit" in his book, **Seven Habits of Highly Effective People.** Steven and I are saying something similar, but I prefer the word creative. For me, it has more depth of meaning. Being creative means that we have accepted the God-given power to think, to plan, and to take responsibility for what happens in our lives.

Creative people are not only pro-active, but they are the architects and designers of their life and business. What distinguishes creative people (the top 10%) from others is that creative people are actively designing (planning) and executing on a daily, weekly, monthly, quarterly, yearly, and on a life-long basis. They never cease to create and re-create their lives.

Creative people alter the structures and patterns in their lives, refusing everywhere to follow old habits and old structures learned in their past. They start with their money habits. Then, they move to their time management patterns. They work on their closest relationships. Then, they sit down with a team of people they have have surrounded themselves with to create new structures and systems which allows all of them to become more of who they can become.

Life is not meant to be lived in survival mode. Life is meant to be lived in abundance. I hope we've arrived at this point together. The theme of this book is *"how you think is more important than the how-to of actions"*.

The top 3% of professionals are the most creative in their life orientation. According to research they are also 10-100 times wealthier than the next 10%. Remember, that less than 10% of our population holds more than 90% of the America's wealth.

Creative people plan, reactive people don't. That's the key difference. That's what distinguishes creative from reactive people. Not only do creative people plan, they continue to plan their lives on an ongoing basis. Not only do they plan, but they commit their plans to writing and take their written plans wherever they go. They review their plans and goals daily. They modify them as needed, and they continue to plan and review throughout life.

I was raised in St. Paul, Minnesota, in St. Louis, Missouri, and in Dubuque, Iowa. What those cities have in common is that they are all on the Mississippi River. I grew up watching the river and its unceasing traffic. Can you imagine the mighty Mississippi without its many locks and dams? I often ask audiences about the reasons for these lock and dams. Some know, others don't. Left to its natural course ("path of least resistance"), the river would flow more at some times of the year than others. The river would be flowing rapidly, and even overflowing in the spring, and would be nearly dry by winter. The tugs and barges that carry massive amounts of coal, oil, grain on the river need 16 feet of draft to navigate. By positioning locks and dams along the river, the seasonal variance in water level can be controlled. The river remains navigable for the entire year, unless the water freezes (which it rarely does anymore).

By installing locks and dams, a new "path of least resistance" is created for the water. New structures alter the flow of water on the Mississippi. This may seem a simple comparison, but money, like water, has a "path of least resistance". Without structures in place to alter the flow, money flows into life in an unpredictable and uncontrolled fashion, and leaves the same way. You make it, you spend it, and it disappears forever.

The time you have is something similar. Some people seem to have far more time than others, yet, time is the most democratic resource known to man. We all have an equal amount of time each day. Some of us are in control of our time, others are not.

The title of this Chapter is, **"Creating Wealth Is Simple But Not Easy!"** It's time to get specific. Some of these things we've touched on before and some are new.

One of the best ways to give yourself a secure future is to plan how you will meet your tax obligations. Many professionals don't do this and the cost to them is tremendous. Think about these guidelines:

- **Federal Income Tax:** It should be no more than 12% of your gross collections.

- **State Income Tax:** It should be no more than 2-4% of your gross collections.

- **F.I.C.A. Tax:** It should be about 1% of your gross collections.

One of the biggest financial advantages you have in owning your own business is the ability to create the most tax-advantaged wealth and freedom plan possible. If you can't do that, you will struggle to create wealth when you are not in control of your tax obligations.

The complexity of the tax code may require that you consult a coordinated team of experts who will work to customize a Wealth and Freedom Plan for you. It's simple, just do it! Would you rather be creating wealth for yourself and your family, or paying excess taxes to the government?

Here's another question to ask yourself: Am I creating wealth, or just consuming what I earn in buying depreciating toys? If you want to overcome the poor habit of failing to save, here are some recommendations. Do everything you can to:

- Structure your business for profit and growth.
- Trade $20,000-$30,000 a year in Federal and State Income Tax for savings and investing in your Wealth and Freedom Plan.
- Re-capture $50,000 to $150,000 a year (depending on your gross revenues) in excess business expenses via the Eight Strategies of the Wealth and Freedom Creator. (It can be more!)
- Find a coordinated wealth creating team who will work with you to customize a wealth plan exclusively for you, your goals, and your future.

The purpose of all these strategies, like the locks and

dams on the Mississippi River, is to restructure the flow of money, in your business and personal life.

At The Schuster Center we spend a considerable amount of our time teaching coordinated Wealth Creating strategies. Some of you will already be familiar with a few of these strategies:

- The Business Blueprint™
- The Profit Creator™
- The Time Treasure™
- The Client Journey™
- The Communication Connection™
- The Attraction Principle™
- The Cash Flow Manager™
- The Freedom Funder™
- The Life Design™

What I want to assure you, based on 30 years of my personal experience, is that these strategies work. You can predictably and reliably change your "path of least resistance" regarding how money flows in your business and life. Keep this little schema in mind:

- **Principles,** that is, foundational, proven truths are used to create **Models,** which generate **Strategies,** which direct your **Actions** that produce the **Outcomes** you desire.

Earlier, I wrote that our lives should not be lived in survival mode. Let me elaborate on that. There are three levels at which we can live our life. We can live at a **survival,** a **success,** or a **significance** level.

It is natural and normal to start one's business in a rather fragile, tentative, fearful state. This is the survival level. If a person stays in survival mode, there is no development nor advancement beyond it. Life, in a survival state, is internally corrosive and leads to emotional disability. It also leads to life disability and business disability.

Beyond survival is success. Success is that level of living in which one strives, works hard, pushes, overachieves, and generally accumulates. Success is typified in the West by accumulation, spending, and consuming more and more. Successful people often sacrifice family and friends for the sake of achieving more. Generally, though not always, individuals who stay at the success level end up crashing. Their health and marriage fail.Other relationships are strained. They drift into drugs or alcohol. They even end up taking their lives. Today, in the United States, there is more depression per capita than there has ever been. If we have so much, why are we so unhappy?

Survival and success are orientations that often dominate the first half of our life. We get a good education, a job, and start making good money. We get promoted, move to the suburbs, go in debt for a big house, buy a couple of foreign cars, and take exotic vacations – all the trappings of keeping-up-with-the-Jones' success. At the success level people live by comparison and in competition with what others have. More is always required to stay in the game.

Significance is the level or stage of life when one moves beyond one's narrow self and self-focused orientation. Significance is the same as what Maslow called *"self-actualization."* In the significance stage, to give, becomes more satisfactory than to receive; to love, more important than being loved. By loving others, one leaves the prison cell of aloneness and isolation that constitutes a state of narcissism and excessive self-interest.

The philosophy behind **The Science of Creating Wealth**™, is that we have a longing to live in abundance. Abundant living can begin at any time. It always begins with a change to a creative from a reactive life orientation. It begins with a plan to live in abundance rather than in scarcity or survival mode. Survival-based and success-oriented individuals are strongly self-centered. They believe that the world revolves around them. They are pre-occupied with getting what they need, often at the expense of others, or at least without concern for the welfare of others.

Creating is not a form of problem solving. Survival-based individuals are locked in a reactive orientation towards money, time, and health, and they rarely spend time or money planning. Planning is the first and constant theme in creating what you want. Planning is indispensable to creating anything. Planning always puts you into the future, rather than reliving the past.

Some people seem to think of wealth as a matter of chance and luck, as if winning the lottery were a typical path to wealth. We know better. Wealth doesn't happen to us by accident. Wealth is something we create in our lives. We cause it to happen by the design and execution of a careful plan.

Many of us may start out in business in something very close to survival mode. This is natural, but it is imperative to get out of survival as soon as possible. This evolution is also a natural step. By nature, we wish to be happy. People in survival are not happy. People who are not happy don't do as well as people who are happy. Happy people live longer lives. They drink less, eat less, and have a more positive outlook in life. In sum, they simply do better than those who are not happy.

A creative orientation toward life and business transcends a reactive and problem solving orientation. The sad truth is that while all human beings have the capacity to evolve or develop, many don't. Some continue to live lives of unquiet desperation and unhappiness.

Some people move beyond survival only to become stuck at the success stage. Fear is the reason. They are fear-based and their fears paralyze them. They are always worried that something will happen to them. They never feel that they have enough money, things, or time. They truly live their entire lives in desperation, in fear, and in scarcity. They are competitive, jealous, and challenging. Seldom satisfied, they seek perfection, not progress.

Significance embodies a different orientation. People

at the level of significance (self-actualized individuals) are happier and more at peace with themselves. Though they continue to plan; their plans more often are about how they can assist or make a difference for others. They become agents of positive change in the world. No longer stuck on themselves, they move into a far freer creative orientation. They are happier, healthier, and live longer in a life they have created.

The earlier in life one can move from survival to success, the sooner one can move on to significance or self-actualization. It is very easy to get stuck at the lower levels in life. Maslow was puzzled, toward the end of his life, about why more Americans were not evolving to higher levels. He wasn't in daily contact with business owners as I've been these past 35 years!

The answer Maslow was looking for has to do with the fact that our culture stimulates most of us to get to the level of success and then stay there. The remedy is to transcend success and move into significance as early in your life as you can.

The Science of Creating Wealth™ is designed to help you get to the level of significance by age 45, assuming you start at about 30. The rest of your life, in fact, your entire life, will be so much better than the life of the average 'reactor'. Leaving behind problems from the lack of money, time and stressful relationships, you will hardly recognize yourself!

Any of us can transform our life by moving from reacting to creating. We can dramatically improve our health by creating health rather than reacting to signs and symptoms of disease. We can dramatically improve our financial health by choosing to create wealth and abundance rather than reacting to money problems. We can dramatically improve our whole experience of living, our entire quality of life, by changing the way we think.

Can we change everything? Of course not. Can we control everything? Of course not. Let me tell you a final secret. *We can control as much as we need to control to create a creative and abundant life.* I am here to help you.

Thank you for reading this book. Many of you have helped me write it. I can honestly say at this point in my life that I get more joy and fulfillment out of watching you transform your lives than I have gotten out of changing my own life. Become a creator of health and wealth, a pursuer of truth and love. Make a difference in the world.

Caritas,
Dr. Michael Schuster ■

The Science of Creating Wealth™

Appendix ■
Some Recent CFPD White Papers
On Creating Wealth

At The Schuster Center, our on-going research and classroom discussions regularly generate study or so-called "white papers" on the topics related to the **Creation of Wealth.** These discussions are often somewhat specialized and technical in nature and resist being absorbed into the chapters of this book. Nevertheless, I thought you might enjoy and profit from reading some of these papers. There follow six recent short papers on topics ranging from median professional incomes to the perils of ultraconservative investing. Feel free to write me about any these topics, or raise them when you are attending a Schuster Center seminar.

(1) Why Doctors Rarely Create Wealth!

Doctors are notorious for making a lot of money (income), living very high lifestyles, but creating little or no wealth. It is critical to define what wealth truly is and how it can be measured and then created.

I'll never forget a lecture I gave on Profitability Management and Wealth Creation in Washington, DC, in December of 1988. A doctor – let's call him Dr. Dan for anonymity sake – walked over to me during the first break with a very enthusiastic look in his eyes. He said, *"My father was a physician and surgeon, and in the 1950's, he was making in excess of $200,000 a year net income; yet, he never would have been able to retire except for the fact that his brother, a common laborer preceded him in death and willed him all of his money."*

He was telling the truth! But how could such a situation come about? There is a great deal of confusion about the difference between high incomes and wealth, and we need to start with definitions and facts.

Here's a definition of wealth that you can take to the bank: *"Wealth is the value of everything you own minus your debts."*

For purposes of studying wealth and the distribution of wealth, economists define wealth in terms of marketable assets such as real estate, stocks and bonds; leaving aside consumer durables such as cars and household items (because they are not as readily converted into cash and are more valuable to home owners for *use* purposes than for resale). Once the value of all marketable assets is determined, then all debts, such as home mortgages and credit card debt are subtracted. The difference is defined as an individual's **net worth.**

In addition, economists use the concept of "financial wealth", which is defined as net worth minus net equity in owner-occupied housing. Financial wealth is a more liquid commodity than marketable wealth, since one's home is often difficult to convert into cash in the short term. Financial wealth is meant to reflect the resources that may be immediately available for consumption in various forms of investments.

It is also clear that we must distinguish wealth from income. Income is what you earn from wages, dividends, interest, and any rents or royalties that are paid to you on properties owned. In theory, those who have high incomes should also be wealthy; but in reality, those at the very top of the wealth distribution often have a high net worth not reflected in income. In short, wealth is not simply a function of your gross business income.

A major fallacy in thinking by professionals who I have counselled these past 30+ years is that of equating high income with wealth. I would say that over 95% of these professionals believe that increasing income means their wealth increases. I'm trying to say that nothing could be farther from the truth.

Doctors and other health-care professionals make

enough money to create wealth – contrast the plight of teachers – but because they don't truly understand what wealth is, they cannot organize their business and their lives to create it. This is tragic waste of a golden opportunity.

Look at wealth distribution. In the United States, wealth is concentrated in relatively few hands. As of 2001, the top 1% of households owned 33.4% of all privately held wealth, and the next 19% of households held 51% of the wealth. That means that 20% of the American population owned a remarkable 84% of the wealth, leaving only 16% for the remaining 80% of the population. These numbers were drawn from the work of Edward Wolff from New York University.

In terms of the narrower concept of financial wealth, the top 1% of households had an even greater share: 39.7%. In terms of financial wealth, the top 1% of households have 44.1% of all privately held stock, 58% of financial securities, and 57.3% of business equity. The top 10% have 85%-90% of the stocks, bonds, trust funds, and business equity, and over 75% of non-home real estate. Since financial wealth, not income or production, is what counts as far as controlling income producing assets, we can say that just 10% of the people own the United States of America.

In my experience of working with professionals and doctors since 1973, I believe that doctors rarely create wealth because they confuse production with creating wealth. They confuse having and living a wonderful lifestyle with creating wealth.

When I started my own practice in 1968, a popular book wrote about the $100,000 practice as a solid goal. By 1975, the same author wrote about the $250,000 practice, and by 1985, the rage was how to build a $500,000 practice. Today ,the buzzword is how to build the $1M practice. Those who reach $1M join groups and clubs whose goal is how to hype themselves up to a $2M practice. The production treadmill is running faster and faster every day. Seems like the more things change, the more they stay the same – or escalate.

Having studied the financial statements and personal net worth of over 10,000 businesses these past years, I can tell you that rarely (less than 1% of the time) do those focusing on production as a way to create wealth succeed in creating wealth. Ninety-nine percent of them fail because they neither understand what true wealth is or because they are working with the wrong methods and models to create wealth.

(2) The Consequences Of Failing To Create Wealth

Many of you have no doubt heard about a famous Harvard study of the consequences of setting or failing to set career and financial goals. In 1979, Harvard asked all its new MBA's about their professional goals. 3% of the MBA's reported having clear written goals and plans, 14% reported having goals and plans but not written ones, and 83% reported no clear goals or plans.

Ten years later, Harvard re-interviewed the same group. 27% of them, all from the no-goals group, currently needed financial assistance and were not self-sufficient. 60% described themselves as living paycheck-to-paycheck. 10% said they are living comfortably, and 3% said they had already achieved financial independence. Those 3% were the exact 3% who had written goals and plans 10 years earlier. Their income from investments and businesses was already ten times greater the total income of the remaining 97%.

The Harvard study actually confirmed an earlier (1953) study from Yale. Yale studied a cross-section of all its graduates and found wealth concentrated in the same small group of about 3%. Every one of these high-income individuals said that they always had written down their career and financial goals.

A first step toward creating wealth is the exercise of sitting down and setting some very dollar-specific and time-specific goals and plans. Goals and plans can be updated and modified as a person moves forward, but the presence of a set of written professional and financial goals seems to be indispensable for a high level of success.

The details of Harvard-Yale studies vividly emphasize that goal setting and planning are a necessity for even the privileged graduates of elite schools. The rate of "no success" among non-goal setters is quite striking.

(3) On The Perils Of Trying To Be Too Safe

When I am speaking to a group about building wealth, I inevitably get a question about whether it is possible to build wealth in a "risk-free" way. The questioner means whether it is possible to build wealth using only so-called "risk-free" instruments like FDIC-insured CD's or U.S. Treasury securities. These instruments are called risk-free, not because they are, literally free of all risks, but because principal and interest are guaranteed by the U.S. Government. The thinking is that the U.S. Government is not going to default on its debt, or if it ever should, no other paper asset is going to be worth much. U.S. Government-insured debt is considered the least risky paper asset you can own.

The answer to this question of whether you can build wealth in a risk-free fashion is not simple. It can't be a simple "yes" or "no" answer. The best answer I can give you is "probably not"; but, I know that answer isn't satisfactory. To give you a better answer, I'm going to have to take you a little way into economics and explain the difference between nominal return and real return. But, before I do that, I want to explain a different problem with "risk-free" investing. It may be just too slow a vehicle for many of you.

When we discussed building wealth by compounding your gains, I gave several examples using monthly increments of $5,000 or $10,000, compounding at a rate of 9%. 9-12% is historically the rate a prudent investor can expect to average if his investments follow the key stock market averages (indexes). 9-12% is not a rate of return available to the risk-free investor. That rate tends to track at around 4-5% historically. The difference between 9% and 5% is the risk premium investors demand and get for putting their funds in uninsured assets like stocks or bonds. The magnitude of this premium continues to surprise economists whose valuations models predict the premium should be about 2.5%.

A businessman who can put $5,000 away per month in an investment account earning 9% will get to nearly a million dollars ($987,100) in ten years. The person getting a 5% return sees a total return of about $200,000 less ($788,100) over that ten-year interval, and he requires 2 years more to get to the million dollar level in investment savings. That's the penalty for "risk-free" savings: $200,000 and two years on the conservative assumptions of our model.

Remember the simple rule for figuring the time it takes your money to double. Divide your rate of return into 72. If your rate is 9%, you double within 8 years. If your rate is 5%, you need 13 years to double. So "risk-free" investing has a substantial time and dollar penalty. Can you afford to pay that penalty?

The Rule of 20 is a benchmark we teach for figuring out a safe level of savings for retirement, or declare financial freedom. You must have saved 20-25 times current annual expenses. Suppose you are a 40-year old professional with very modest expenses of $100,000 annually. Your freedom number is $2,000,000. Putting away $5,000 per month at 5%, you are 20 years away from that goal. Are you willing to commit to that amount of work time in order to reach your goal – 240 more months? If you aren't, you need to be in an environment to save and invest at a higher rate of return.

The Science of Creating Wealth™

But, there is also another and a greater problem to "risk-free" investing, and it has to do with the distinction I spoke of at the beginning. Inflation is the arch-enemy of anyone saving and investing conservatively to create wealth. Inflation means the costs of goods and services rise rapidly. In the first quarter of 2007, the so-called "core rate" of inflation was a tame 2.6%; but, many components of our budget, absent or underestimated by this official number, things (food, housing, healthcare and transportation), pushed the real rate of inflation most consumers were facing to around 6%.

If your money is "safely" earning 5% while the foods and services you must buy are rising at 6% or more there is a huge problem in your investment strategy. Your *real* rate of return equals the nominal, or stated rate, minus the rate of inflation. In this case, your *real* rate of return is a (minus) -1%. You are losing 1% of your purchasing power per year.

It is pretty obvious that creating wealth requires you to sustain and compound a positive rate of *real* growth. Real growth is more important than any nominal rate. I remember in 1980, when one could buy 17% U.S. Treasury bills. But, inflation was so out of control at that point that a 17% return probably represented no real growth. The Feds have vowed that will not happen again. We all hope that is the case.

Some economists say 2-3% real growth is sufficient for long-term saving. I think that is on the low side, at least, if you want to create financial freedom on a ten year horizon. I recommend that you target 4-5% real growth per year. So long as inflation does not heat up again, a 9-12% return meets or exceeds this goal. But a 5% "risk-free" return represents essentially no growth; or, the most meager growth in real terms. "Risk-free" instruments guarantee you the return of your principal with interest, but they don't guarantee you any real growth, which is the reason you are saving and investing.

So, the problem with "risk-free" investments are not just that they compound too slowly; but, they cost you money and time. The more serious problem is that they don't let you experience any real growth. Or, perhaps, if inflation dips suddenly, you only realize a 1-2% real growth.

Therefore, the instruments touted as the safest you can own are, in fact, one of the riskiest. If risk measures the probability, you will not be able to achieve your goal. So, trying to create wealth with CD's can be a potentially, very risky business.

(4) Why Many Professionals Fail To Build Wealth

Fifty years ago, the Nobel laureate economist Milton Friedman published a theory on wealth and consumption that has become the basis for banks lending to professionals. The *Permanent Income Hypothesis (PIH),* says that higher income individuals will base their present rate of consumption on an estimate of their lifetime income. They spend annually a fairly constant percentage of what they estimate their lifetime income will be.

They regard their lifetime income, distributed evenly over their working life, to be their "permanent income", and plan and act accordingly. In windfall years, they save more; in bad years, they spend a little less; but they stay on track, based on expected lifetime income. Because most of them also tend to estimate their lifetime income conservatively, they consume less, save more, and build wealth.

Lower income individuals, by contrast, are much more Keynesian in their consumption. They spend based on their current income; consuming much more in windfall years, and much less in lean years – with no buffering expectation of a permanent lifetime income. Tending to consume *all* of their disposable income (or more, if easy lending allows it), they also have no resources left for building wealth.

Banks and lenders, the PIH suggests, should recognize and support these two different attitudes toward consumption. Loans to lower income individuals should be based tightly on current income and debt, taking into consideration just their ability to repay over the term of loan. For professionals, especially young professionals, the rules should be different. Look at their lifetime potential, assume current income will soon rise to that level, and lend based on lifetime potential.

Bankers, in fact, believe in the PIH. Several years ago, a young dental specialist I knew was able to finance a new home, office and car in one visit to the local bank. The loan officer barely looked at his current financials, which would not have passed even for the car by the standard rules of lending. But, he was a young, attractive dental specialist, setting up in an affluent community. He was good for it! We all could tell such stories.

Research over the past fifty years, has tended to confirm much of the PIH. One conspicuous exception, however, has been the assumption that higher income people have a "propensity to conservatively estimate their permanent income". It now seems apparently clear that many professionals do not base their consumption on a *conservative* estimate of their lifetime or permanent income. They seriously overestimate their lifetime earnings, based primarily on an unrealistic estimate of their working life *("I can work until I drop")*. They also spend too high a percentage of that estimated lifetime income on an annual basis. The result is they often end up like lower income workers, overconsuming, failing to save, and encountering serious financial challenges later in life, or whenever income is disrupted. Bankers and lenders aid and abet this problem in the case of professionals by easy lending that accepts the assumptions of a longer work life and a higher rate of consumption.

Bank lending has tightened somewhat in recent years, but lending to professionals is still probably far too easy for everyone's good. Friedman's PIH offers us a vision of how higher income people SHOULD regulate their consumption and create (build) wealth. Unfortunately, it assumes a propensity to conservatively estimate lifetime income and favor saving over consuming. The culture in which we live does not encourage conservative financial habits. Conspicuous consumption is celebrated, not careful saving and investing. A great many younger professionals fall into this trap and fail to create (build) wealth despite high incomes.

The Science of Creating Wealth™

The remedy implicit in the PIH is that professionals must be counselled to take a careful and conservative look at their (remaining) expected work life and lifetime income. A healthy young man or woman coming out of dental or other professional schools may have an expected work life of about 35-40 years; but, many will become disabled long before then.

A young dentist's net income over the next ten years, according to National Labor statistics, is likely to average $135,000 to $180,000. Put in a conservative estimate of what you believe to be *your* remaining lifetime income, factor in debt, and a healthy rate of saving, and see what a realistic, reasonable rate of consumption is for you.

To create wealth, professionals do not need to become miserly consumers, but the lessons of the PIH are clear. With the best intention,s in terms of financial prudence, bankers may over lend and professionals may over consume.

(5) Why American Consumers Fail To Create Wealth

Americans in 2005 spent 100.5% of their after-tax income, achieving the lowest rate of savings in the U.S. since 1933m and the lowest rate of savings by far among the industrialized nations. Europeans and Asians average a 10-14% rate of savings. In recent years, America has struggled to achieve any positive rate of savings.

It is impossible to build wealth without a positive rate of savings, and the recent European-Asian experience suggests that the rate of savings needs to be at minimum double-digit.

The model developed in **The Science of Creating Wealth**™ proposes that professionals try to target 15% of their production as savings. The before-tax equivalent of 15% of production is hard to estimate, but it may represent about 25-30% of taxable income as savings. Countries without a robust economy, like Italy, manage to save at this rate, so it is a very feasible. A generation of non-saving Americans is going to be in deep trouble at retirement age.

American households (2004) have an average debt of $84,454, equal to nearly two years of after tax income. 18% of that debt is credit card, installment loans and other high interest consumer debt.

Not all debt is bad, as **The Science of Creating Wealth**™ concedes, but all high interest consumer debt is bad and should be eliminated. Professionals should not carry any high interest consumer debt. Credit card and other such debts compound *against you* at 22% per annum. No investments can offset that level of drain on your income.

Americans spend about 17-19% of their income to service debt, and that percentage is rising (median ratio of debt to income, 1998-2006). A quarter of those debt payments are to service credit card debt.

The Science of Creating Wealth™ addressed the effect of losing potential investment dollars to servicing debt. 15-20% of your income lost to debt is far too much. It seriously compromises your ability to create wealth through compounding investment dollars. Even if mortgage debt is unavoidable, 10%

of your income lost to servicing debt is an achievable upper bound for professionals.

The average American (FED RES 2004) has a net worth of $93,000. $28,000 of it is in financial assets. Americans at retirement are worth less, perhaps substantially less. The average American is trying to retire on savings equal to about 180 days of average income.

Spending and not saving has a predictable result. The Federal Reserve thinks the average American has a net worth of $93,000, but other estimates of the personal wealth of Americans arrive at a number half that size. **The Science of Creating Wealth**™ recommends that professionals target 20-25x their average income as a safe retirement/financial freedom benchmark. Americans with $28,000 saved at retirement have a half-year of income saved. Their odds of falling into poverty in retirement are very high. Americans need to consume less, reduce debt, and save more if they have any hope of a safe and comfortable retirement.

(6) Creating Wealth Is Not A Matter Of Luck

There is a well-respected view that says we are all condemned to be average, or at least nearly so, in terms of the financial rewards we can reap from our professional efforts. The foundations of this view are two economic principles that are not obviously wrong.

The first, says that any marketplace in which there is an adequate supply of some professional service will impose a fairly narrow valuation on that service. In simplest terms, the marketplace will price the service and do so rather precisely (maybe at certain tiers, but that is complication we can ignore for now).

The second principle, is that the market will also set a limit to how frequently a provider may deliver those services. The professional may offer his services as often as he chooses, but the competitive market will absorb only so much of his services at the competitive price.

Together these principles predict that economic forces are very strong in containing the compensation of professionals within a fairly narrow range. The resulting distribution of income for any such profession will strongly resemble the familiar Bell Curve or Normal distribution, with 95% of all incomes distributed closely and symmetrically about the average or mean value.

A popular financial and career website (HR Data 2006) reports exactly such a Bell curve distribution for dental incomes:

- **The average (mean) income for dentists in the US (2006) was $135,279.**
- **68% of all dentists earn between $115,000 and $156,000**
- **95% of all dentists earned between $93,000 and $177,000.**
- **99.7% of all dentists earned between $71,000 and $199,000.**

Similar distributions appear for all the other higher income professions.

Never mind the suspect accuracy of dollars values that are being assigned. Think about the shape of the distribution of incomes. You all remember hearing about the Bell Curve in Stats 101. A Bell Curve means dental incomes as distributed symmetrically or "normally" about an average value of around $135,000. 95.4% of all dental professional incomes are said to lie within a fairly narrow range of either $42,000 above or $42,000 below this average. Only 2.3% of dental professionals manage to exceed about $177,000 a year according this distribution.

A distribution of this sort is touted as strong confirmation for the economic view we mentioned at the beginning. You see why. How else can we explain the narrow and orderly grouping of incomes about a single average, unless that average reflects the marketplace's tight valuation of this service? A professional may do a little better, or a little worse, than the average, but the variation is going to be small enough to be accounted for by chance. Indeed, this is the same distribution that describes games of chance.

So if professional incomes are normal distribution, that would be a clear indication that **economic forces conspire to keep all professionals close to the average,** at least in terms of the compensation they can earn. A professional may be significantly above normal in his clinical skills or in his business practices. Nevertheless, market forces constitute a formidable barrier to his raising his income into the top brackets.

This is a pretty pessimistic view, isn't it? Powerful

economic forces oppose our efforts to move beyond average. We can work very hard to improve our skills and improve our business, but it's not clear that the marketplace will let us break away.

Well, fortunately, there is a serious problem with the "evidence" of the normal distribution of professional incomes. The income data we just looked at is actually NOT CORRECT. It is a misrepresentation of the data. A lie, if you prefer plainer speaking. It has been known to economists for many years that **professional incomes are not normally or symmetrically distributed about an average value.** Many forms of employment do show nearly normal distributions, but professional incomes markedly do not.

A more accurate representation of professional incomes shows a distribution that is noticeably skewed to the right (higher incomes), with a much longer and fatter right tail. Can you visualize this? The upper 10% of the curve in particular is more than twice the size of a normal distribution. This reflects the fact the income range of the top 10% of professionals is very wide and improbably above the mean, if the mean were thought to be some market-determined "fair" rate of compensation from which only minor variation can be expected. In fact, the incomes of the top 10% of professionals significantly raise the mean instead of contributing negligibly to it.

Dentists, as we said, are no exception. This right skewing of the income distribution is attested throughout the professions – medicine, law, and education – including dentistry. The top 10% always manage to earn incomes that far exceed the average. Economists accept that this kind distribution cannot be explained on a model that offers only a market-determined mean and chance variation from it. Some other force or forces are creating the remarkable income distribution of professionals.

A recent (2000) study by two economists, Bouchard and Mezard, looks for these forces and argues that it is precisely the **wealth-creating efforts** of top professionals that skew the income curve. The top 10%, and especially the top 5%, divert significant amounts of their professional income into business asset building investments. This, in turn, accelerates the growth of their income from these investments in a kind of wealth-building upward spiral. The Bouchard and Mezard model has won confirmation in the work of Sourna (2002) and others, and continues to be developed. The hallowed view that professional incomes are narrowly constrained and determined by market forces has, perhaps, finally been laid to rest. ∎

How Do You Prepare For A Retirement That Could Last Longer Than The Years Spent Working?

Now that you have completed **The Science of Creating Wealth**™, I'd like to share with you the most important thing you can do for yourself, your family, your business and your life. And that is to create a comprehensive, integrated plan.

Only 3% of professionals that I have met these past 30 years have a *Written Plan* that coordinates **business income, personal income, taxes, retirement planning, savings** and **investments.**

- Step One is creating the plan.
- Step Two is executing the plan.

To secure a complimentary first hour discussion about your future, please complete (print clearly) the following form with the information requested and return to:

THE SCHUSTER CENTER
9312 E. Raintree Drive
Scottsdale, Arizona 85260
www.schustercenter.com

Or, call Toll Free 1.800.288.9393 and secure a private discussion regarding *"Creating a Wealth and Freedom Plan*™*"*. I'll send you two reports: **"Tied To The Chair"** and **"Freedom From The Chair."**

Yes, I have read **The Science of Creating Wealth**™, and I would like to participate in a complimentary discussion regarding my business, my life plan and my future.

My name is_____

My address is:

Street _____

City _____

State_____Zip _____

My phone is_____

Contact person _____

E-mail _____

I have owned my business for_____ years.

My key concerns are:

Net profit _____High taxes _____

Tax deferred savings _____

Not enough personal income _____

I want an integrated plan _____

A trusted partner to help me execute my plan_____

Finding Staff _____ Finding patients/clients _____

THE SCHUSTER CENTER • **Schuster's Performance Coach, Inc.** • **www.schustercenter.com**
9312 East Raintree Drive • Scottsdale, AZ 85260 • 1.800.288.9393 • Fax: 480.970.2498

The Science of Creating Wealth™

— NOTES —

— NOTES —

The Science of Creating Wealth™

— NOTES —

— NOTES —

The Science of Creating Wealth™